Israel

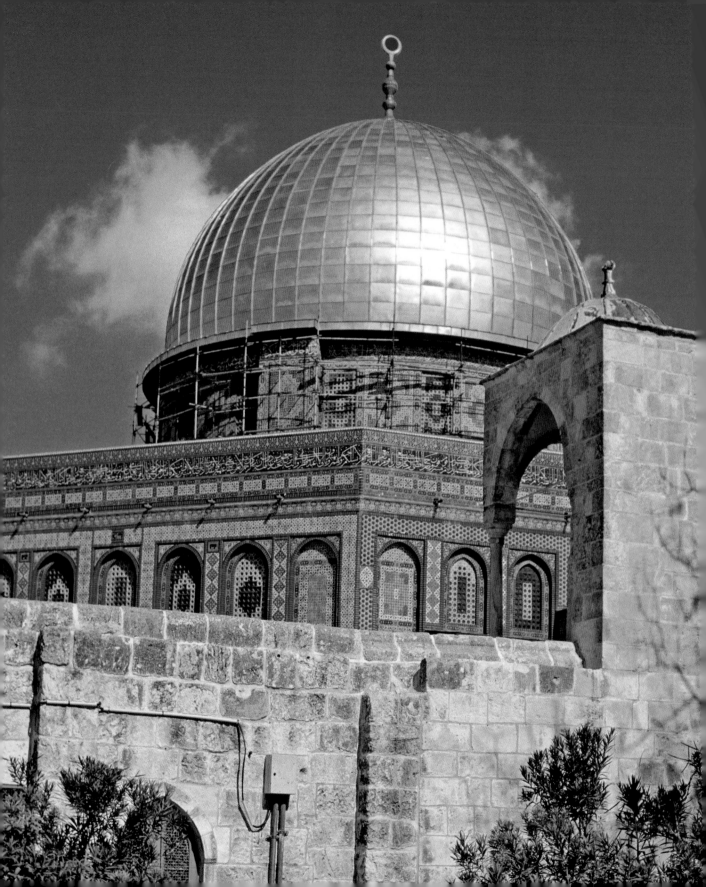

Israel

BY NEL YOMTOV

Enchantment of the World™
Second Series

Children's Press®

An Imprint of Scholastic Inc.

NEW YORK   TORONTO   LONDON   AUCKLAND   SYDNEY
MEXICO CITY   NEW DELHI   HONG KONG
DANBURY, CONNECTICUT

Frontispiece: The Dome of the Rock, Jerusalem

Consultant: Kamran Agahaie, Director of the Center for Middle Eastern Studies, University of Texas–Austin

Please note: All statistics are as up-to-date as possible at the time of publication.

Book production by The Design Lab

Library of Congress Cataloging-in-Publication Data

Yomtov, Nelson.
  Israel/by Nel Yomtov.
      p. cm.—(Enchantment of the world)
  Includes bibliographical references and index.
  ISBN-13: 978-0-531-25313-7 (lib. bdg.)
  ISBN-10: 0-531-25313-9 (lib. bdg.)
  1. Israel—Juvenile literature. 2. Israel—Description and travel—Juvenile literature. I. Title.
    II. Series.
  DS118.Y66 2011
  956.94—dc23   2011031122

Israel

Contents

Cover photo:
A statue in the
Negev Desert

Dead Sea

Israeli gazelle

Israel Today

ISRAEL IS SMALL FOR A NATION, BUT IT IS UNMATCHED in complexity, diversity, and controversy. Its geography ranges from bone-dry deserts to lush farmland to thick forests to towering, snowcapped mountains. The landscape of its cities features ancient biblical sites sitting next to modern, gleaming skyscrapers. People from more than one hundred countries live in Israel, providing this tiny sliver of land with the influences of almost every race, culture, religion, and lifestyle found in the world. This region's political and cultural history spans three thousand years, yet Israel only became a nation in 1948. It is a country in which the conflict between Palestinians and Jews at times seems destined to rage forever. Despite this conflict, Israel aspires to be a melting pot of hope and opportunity for all its people.

Opposite: **The population of Tel Aviv has grown from two thousand in 1920 to more than four hundred thousand today.**

Town and Country

Most Israelis live in urban areas located along Israel's coast on the Mediterranean Sea. Modern cities such as Tel Aviv, Haifa, and Ashdod hum with activity. High-rise apartment

complexes, museums, office buildings, and theaters make these cities the equal of most urban areas in the world. Away from the large cities, Israelis have turned parts of the barren Negev Desert into fertile farmland. Israel's pioneering spirit has made the nation a leading producer of fruits, vegetables, flowers, and other agricultural products. Grape vineyards and banana and date groves are found throughout the country, yielding produce for consumers around the world.

Grapes are one of the many crops grown in Israel.

A Center of Religion

Israel is sacred ground for three of the world's major religions: Judaism, Christianity, and Islam. In Jerusalem, which is the capital of Israel, the holiest sites of each religion stand side by side. The Second Temple was the center of Jewish religious life between 516 BCE and 70 CE. The Romans destroyed the temple, leaving only what remains today: the Western Wall, still an important site for Jewish prayer. Not far from the Western Wall is one of Christianity's holiest shrines, the Church of the Holy Sepulchre. Jesus Christ, who Christians believe was the son of God, is said to have been crucified and buried on this site. Nearby is Islam's Dome of the Rock and al-Aqsa Mosque, which were built more than thirteen hundred years ago, following the Muslim conquest of Jerusalem. It is believed to be the place where the Prophet Muhammad, who first spread the word about Islam, rose into heaven.

A Clash of Beliefs

Israelis honor and respect their ancient history, but they are a people who must live in the harsh realities of the present. Modern Israel was created as an independent state in 1948, as a haven and spiritual homeland for Jews. Facing discrimination and violence abroad, millions of Jews flocked to Israel

David Ben-Gurion, Israel's first prime minister, reads Israel's declaration of independence on May 14, 1948.

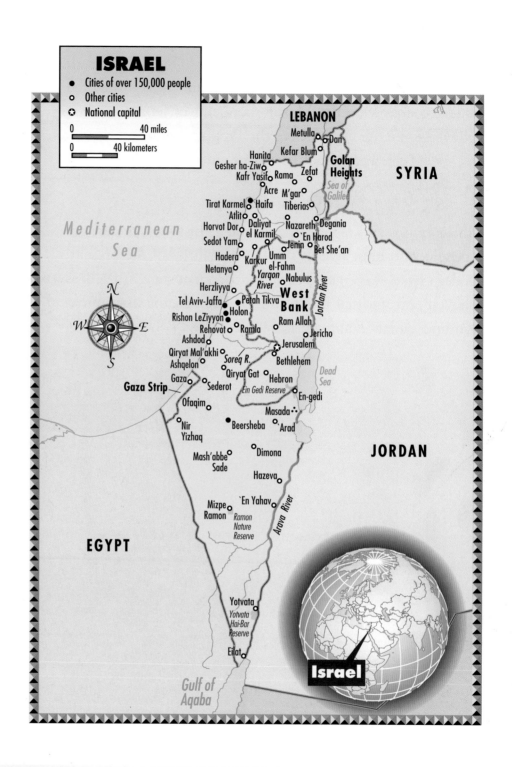

ISRAEL

- ● Cities of over 150,000 people
- ○ Other cities
- ✪ National capital

0   40 miles

0   40 kilometers

LEBANON

SYRIA

Metulla
Dan
Hanita
Kefar Blum
Gesher ha-Ziw
Kafr Yasif
Rama
Zefat
Golan Heights
Acre
M'gar
Sea of Galilee
Tirat Karmel
Haifa
Tiberias
Atlit
Horvot Dor
Daliyat el Karmil
Nazareth
Degania
Sedot Yam
`En Harod
Jenin
Bet She'an
Hadera
Karkur
Umm el-Fahm
Netanya
Yarqon River
Nabulus
Herzliyya
Jordan River
Tel Aviv-Jaffa
Petah Tikva
West Bank
Holon
Rishon LeZiyyon
Ram Allah
Rehovot
Ramla
Jericho
Ashdod
Jerusalem
Qiryat Mal'akhi
Soreq R.
Bethlehem
Ashqelon
Dead Sea
Qiryat Gat
Gaza Strip
Gaza
Hebron
Sederot
Ein Gedi Reserve
En-gedi
Ofaqim
Masada
JORDAN
Nir Yizhaq
Beersheba
Arad
Mash'abbe Sade
Dimona
Hazeva
`En Yahav
Mizpe Ramon
Ramon Nature Reserve
Arava River

EGYPT

Mediterranean Sea

N
W   E
S

Yotvata
Yotvata Hai-Bar Reserve

Eilat

Gulf of Aqaba

Israel

to start life anew. The same year as its creation, Israel fought a war with its Arab neighbors, who opposed the creation of a Jewish state in the area. At that time, the area was called Palestine, and Palestinian Arabs constituted a majority of the population. Some anti-Israeli governments in the Middle East—notably Egypt, Jordan, Morocco, Tunisia, and Turkey—have resumed diplomatic relations with Israel. But many other Middle Eastern governments have not and remain hostile toward Israel. Several wars and smaller military conflicts have been fought since 1948.

Today, Israeli-Palestinian relations are strained and uneasy. The region that is now Israel has been home to Palestinians for many centuries. When Israel was established, hundreds of thousands of Palestinians fled the region to escape the violence of the war. Many went to other Arab countries, while others settled in the West Bank, a region along the Jordan River; in the Golan Heights in northern Israel; or in the Gaza Strip on Israel's Mediterranean coast. Some of these refugees and their descendants became citizens of these Arab states. Others moved to different parts of the world. Still others remain in refugee camps today. Violent conflicts between Palestinians and Israeli Jewish citizens and the Israeli army have occurred for decades along these points and others.

Despite the differences among Israel's peoples, they share the common experience of building the nation. Regardless of their political leanings or religious beliefs, there is a kinship among them that will perhaps heal the wounds of old. Until then, Israel must remain a place of optimism and tolerance.

A Diverse Landscape

ISRAEL IS A SMALL, WEDGE-SHAPED NATION THAT IS part of the Middle East, the region that includes western Asia and northern Africa. Sitting at the junction of the two continents, Israel's western border is formed by the Mediterranean Sea. Lebanon lies to the north, and Syria lies to the northeast. Jordan occupies the eastern border of Israel, and Egypt is to the southwest. Israel's southernmost area reaches to the Gulf of Aqaba and the Red Sea.

Opposite: **Salt crystals line the edge of the Dead Sea. The Dead Sea is 8.6 times saltier than the ocean, making it one of the world's saltiest bodies of water.**

A Tiny Nation

Israel is 263 miles (423 kilometers) long from north to south, and its width varies from 71 miles (114 km) at its widest point to 9.3 miles (15 km) at its narrowest. The tiny nation occupies just 8,522 square miles (22,072 square kilometers), making it slightly larger than the state of New Jersey.

The land of Israel, or Eretz Israel, includes East Jerusalem, which is part of the West Bank; the Golan Heights, which today is part of Syria but controlled by Israel; and a portion of the Sinai Peninsula, which is now part of Egypt. All of these territories have been under the control of the Israeli government at one time or another. East Jerusalem was annexed to Israel in 1967. Also since 1967, Israel has controlled the Golan Heights of Syria, and thousands of Jewish Israelis have moved into settlements there. The Sinai was similarly controlled between 1967 and 1973.

The status of the West Bank has changed over time. The Israeli government still controls the entire West Bank, but the Palestinian Authority works there as a semi-government, although under Israeli military control. This situation is complex, because over the past few decades, hundreds of thousands

The Israeli settlement of Bnei Yehuda was established in the Golan Heights in 1972.

Israel's Geographic Features

Area: 8,522 square miles (22,072 sq km)

Highest Elevation: Mount Meron, 3,963 feet (1,208 m) above sea level

Lowest Elevation: Dead Sea, 1,388 feet (423 m) below sea level

Longest River: Jordan River, 199 miles (320 km)

Largest Lake: Sea of Galilee, 64 square miles (166 sq km)

Largest City: Jerusalem, population 773,700 (2010 est.)

Highest Recorded Temperature: 129°F (54°C), at Tirat Zvi, June 21, 1942

Lowest Recorded Temperature: 7.3°F (–13.7°C), at Tel Hatanim, February 7, 1950

Average Temperatures: January: 43°F to 59°F (6°C to 15°C); August: 72°F to 91°F (22°C to 33°C)

Average Annual Rainfall: 1.2 inches (3 cm) in the south; 35 inches (89 cm) in the north

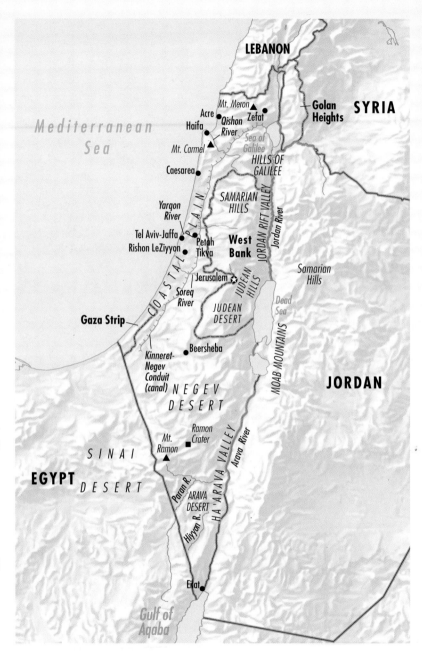

The rocky Hills of Galilee rise to heights of about 4,000 feet (1,200 m).

of Jewish Israelis have moved into the West Bank. They live in settlements that are separated from the Palestinian populations. Gaza, which Israel has controlled since 1967, has experienced a similar pattern, but over the past few years Israel has withdrawn all Jewish Israeli settlements from the area.

The Lay of the Land

Israel can be divided into five main geographical regions. They are the Hills of Galilee in the north, the Jordan Rift Valley in the east, the Negev Desert in the south, the narrow coastal plain in the west, and the Samarian and Judean Hills in the center of the country.

The Hills of Galilee are home to Mount Meron, Israel's highest peak, which is located in Upper Galilee. To the south lies Lower Galilee, with fertile valley farmland. Farther south, the hills fall sharply to the Sea of Galilee, also known as Lake Kinneret.

The Jordan Rift Valley forms a long, thin strip along Israel's eastern border. It is part of a 4,000-mile (6,500 km) valley system that runs from Syria through East Africa. The Jordan River runs through the Hula Valley, a rich agricultural area where fruit orchards and cotton fields abound. The Golan Heights overlooks the valley. To the south, the Jordan River flows into the Sea of Galilee and then continues southward to drain into the Dead Sea. The Rift Valley runs farther through the Arava, a narrow stretch of desert, and then continues to the Red Sea near the Gulf of Aqaba.

The rocky Negev Desert in the south covers about 60 percent of Israel. Forming the shape of an upside-down triangle, the 4,700-square-mile (12,200 sq km) Negev is dotted with cliffs, mountains, dry riverbeds, and deep craters and canyons. The heart-shaped Ramon Crater is one of the world's largest craters, measuring 25

The Jordan River forms part of the border between Israel and Jordan.

miles (40 km) long and 1,600 feet (500 m) deep. The crater and the surrounding land form the Ramon Nature Reserve, Israel's largest national park. The city of Beersheba in the northern Negev is the largest in the area. In the extreme south, on the Gulf of Aqaba, lies the town of Eilat, a popular tourist spot.

The entire Negev region is arid, with average rainfall varying between 12 inches (30 centimeters) in the north and only 2 inches (5 cm) on the Jordanian border. In this small nation, where every acre of land needs to be used, modern agricultural developments and large-scale irrigation projects have trans-

A kite surfer glides atop the Red Sea near Eilat.

formed the Negev into productive farmland. The Negev now produces about 40 percent of Israel's vegetables and field crops.

Israel's western coastal plain runs along the eastern shore of the Mediterranean Sea. Many small rivers flow through the plain, making the region one of Israel's most productive agricultural areas. The coastal plain is also Israel's largest industrialized area. Major cities include Tel Aviv, the principal port city of Haifa, and the historic ancient towns of Acre and Caesarea. The coastal plain is home to about 60 percent of Israel's population.

Jerusalem spreads across the Judean Hills.

The Samarian and Judean Hills in the center of the country lie mainly in the Israeli-controlled West Bank. Israel's capital, Jerusalem, is located in the rocky Judean Hills. The ancient towns of Hebron and Bethlehem on the West Bank are significant for their religious importance to Jews, Christians, and Muslims.

Rivers and Lakes

The Jordan River, Israel's longest, flows 199 miles (320 km) southward from the mountains of Lebanon and Syria through Israel and into the Dead Sea. The Jordan supplies Israel with about 40 percent of its fresh water, which is used for drinking and irrigation. The Yarqon River, Israel's second-largest river,

The Sea of Galilee is used for both recreation and fishing.

flows through the central, most populated part of the country before emptying into the Mediterranean Sea.

Lying in the Jordan Rift Valley near the Golan Heights, the Sea of Galilee is the largest freshwater lake in Israel, measuring 13 miles (21 km) long and 8 miles (13 km) wide. The Greeks and Romans built several thriving settlements near the Galilee. The New Testament describes how Jesus walked on the waters of the Galilee. The first kibbutz, or cooperative farming community, was founded near the Galilee in 1909 by Jewish settlers. The Galilee is a major tourist spot, attracting many Christian pilgrims who visit the spiritual sites in nearby areas.

The Dead Sea, which forms part of the border between Israel and Jordan, is the saltiest body of water on earth. Its waters are nearly ten times as salty as ocean water. Located

1,388 feet (423 meters) below sea level, the Dead Sea is also the lowest lake on earth.

The lake contains many other minerals, including magnesium, iodine, bromine, and potash, which are taken from the lake for industrial uses. The heavy concentration of minerals makes it almost impossible to dive beneath the water's surface. Swimmers can easily float in the Dead Sea. The Dead Sea got its name because the minerals prevent life-forms other than bacteria from surviving in the waters.

Climate

Israel has two seasons. The rainy winter period lasts from November through March, and a dry summer season lasts from April through October. Climates vary significantly in different areas throughout the country.

Northern Israel is usually cooler than the southern region. Mountainous areas, such as those surrounding Jerusalem, tend to be cooler than low-lying areas. The Jordan Rift Valley,

Why So Salty?

The Dead Sea is fed by rivers and streams flowing down from the mountains that surround it. But no rivers drain out of the Dead Sea. Water escapes the sea only by evaporation. When the water evaporates, it leaves behind the minerals that have dissolved in the water, including salt. The accumulating salt gets trapped within the Dead Sea's shores, and the sea gets saltier and saltier with each passing day.

Snow coats the ground near an ancient synagogue on Mount Meron.

sitting below sea level, experiences high temperatures all year. Rainfall is heaviest in the north, west, and center of the country. The Hills of Galilee in the northwest experience the heaviest amounts of rainfall, receiving 46 inches (117 cm) yearly.

January is the coldest month of the year, with average temperatures ranging from 43 to 59 degrees Fahrenheit (6 to 15 degrees Celsius) nationwide. In summer, breezes generally cool northern Israel, but southern desert regions can reach temperatures of 120°F (49°C).

Although snow is rare in most of Israel, every year snow falls on Mount Meron, Israel's northernmost point, in the Golan Heights. Rising 3,963 feet (1,208 m) high, Meron is Israel's highest point and the site of the nation's only ski resort, on Mount Hermon.

Israel experiences extreme weather conditions that include sandstorms, droughts, and flash floods. Hot desert winds carrying dust and sand often kick up suddenly, usually from October to May. The winds lower humidity and raise temperatures and air pollution levels to unhealthy levels. Flash floods can occur in the dry Negev when rare, heavy rainfalls fill arid riverbeds with fast-moving water. The surging rainwater can be highly dangerous—killing people, destroying property, overflowing dams, and wiping out communication lines.

Looking at Israel's Cities

Tel Aviv (right), Israel's second-largest city, has a population of 403,700, including the neighboring ancient community of Jaffa. Founded in 1909 by sixty families as a Jewish neighborhood, Tel Aviv has blossomed to become Israel's business and cultural center. The Tel Aviv Stock Exchange and the Diamond Exchange are two of the city's most important financial institutions. The city is also home to the Tel Aviv Performing Arts Center and the Fredric R. Mann Auditorium, also known as the Culture Palace. Both offer world-class performances of dance, theater, classical music, opera, and fine arts exhibitions. With its clean, white beaches and bustling neighborhoods that offer shopping, fine restaurants, and a busy nightlife, Tel Aviv has earned the nickname the "city that never stops."

The earliest mention of the city of Haifa dates to the third century BCE. Haifa today has a population of 265,600. It is an important port and home to many factories and high-tech industries that have experienced a major boom. Important landmarks include the Baha'i Gardens and World Center, the Hecht Museum on the campus of the University of Haifa, and the National Museum of Science. Haifa is home to Jews, Muslims, Christian Arabs, Ahmadis, Druze, Baha'is, and members of other religious groups. It is one of the Middle East's most diverse communities.

Rishon LeZiyyon (The First to Zion), located just south of Tel Aviv, is Israel's fourth-largest city, with a population of 228,200. The city was founded in 1882 by European Jewish immigrants as the first Jewish settlement in Israel. In 1886, the first school to use Hebrew as the official language of instruction was established there. Today, Rishon LeZiyyon is a center for construction, the wine industry, and commerce.

Petah Tikva (Opening of Hope) was founded in 1878 by European Jews on what was originally swampland. The city has blossomed into the fifth-largest in Israel, with a population of 209,600 in 2010. It's the second-largest industrial center in the nation, after Haifa. Petah Tikva's major businesses include textiles, processed foods, plastics, tires and rubber products, and high-tech and communications industries. The Petah Tikva Museum Complex features several museums and cultural attractions, most notably the Museum of Art, which showcases works of contemporary art by Israeli and international artists.

CHAPTER
THREE

ISRAEL IS HOME TO A DIVERSE RANGE OF PLANT AND animal life. The tiny nation serves as the bridge between a temperate zone of the Mediterranean Sea and a tropical zone of desert land. Within its borders are fertile fields, woodlands, arid deserts, snowcapped mountains, and vast sand dunes. This broad range of geography and climate plays host to roughly forty-seven thousand species of plants and animals.

Opposite: **Nineteen species of irises grow wild in Israel. They brighten the hillsides from January to April.**

Plant Life

Israel's distribution of flowers and plants changes with its different geographic and climatic zones. Hilly regions of the north are filled with lush woodlands of oak trees. Colorful shrubs such as thorny broom and rockrose erupt in vibrant pinks and yellows when they bloom in spring. By December, hyacinths, crocuses, and narcissi cover the hillsides. Irises, tulips, and daisies appear soon after. Large plane trees, grown for their beauty, thrive along the freshwater streams of Galilee.

In the east, rainfall in the Rift Valley increases as one travels northward. A sparse woodland of low bush and scrub, with trees generally no taller than 13 feet (4 m), covers the sands of the Arava River valley. Long-rooted Sudanese trees grow in oases in the hot regions of the Arava, the Dead Sea, and the Jordan River valley, where runoff and underground water collect. Oases also appear around Jericho near the West Bank, where similar types of trees can thrive.

Trees flourish in an oasis near Jericho.

The dry southern region of the Negev generally supports only plants that can survive with little water. Thorny acacia trees and sabra cactus are common in the area. The sabra cactus was imported from Arizona and New Mexico in the nineteenth century. It produces a prickly pear, which is eaten widely throughout Israel. Higher regions of the Negev support pistachio trees and date palm trees. Atlantic pistachio trees can grow up to 40 feet (12 m) high and live up to one thousand years.

In the west, a successful program of replanting trees has replenished the coastal plain forest, which had been cut down over the centuries. Many of the Mediterranean woodlands have been turned into olive groves.

Acacia trees are one of the few types of trees that grow in the Negev.

The horns of male Nubian ibexes can reach 3 feet (1 m) long.

Mammals

Israel is home to 116 species of mammals. The nation's largest mammals are the gazelle, the Nubian ibex, the wild boar, and the fox. The mountain gazelle lives in the northern two-thirds of the country, and the Negev gazelle lives in the southern desert regions. Both species live in the region of the Dead Sea. The Nubian ibex is a type of wild goat that lives mainly in the Negev and Judean Deserts. Ibex are extremely agile climbers, moving easily up and down steep cliffs and slopes. They feed on desert grasses and shrubs.

Smaller mammals include porcupines, hedgehogs, badgers, martens, and Egyptian mongooses. The Syrian rock hyrax is a rabbit-size hoofed animal that lives throughout Israel.

Five mammals live only in Israel. They include four species of mole rat and the Negev shrew.

Birdlife

Birds abound throughout Israel because the country is located on the migration route from Europe and western Asia to Africa. Because the flow of bird traffic is so heavy, aircraft are often prohibited from flying in migration paths.

Some songbirds such as the bulbul, the Sylvia warbler, and the goldcrest live in Israel year-round. Migrant species include honey buzzards and pelicans. Coots and starlings spend winters in Israel feeding on farmland and fish farms.

Eagles, falcons, hawks, and kestrels also make their home in Israel, but hunting has significantly reduced their numbers.

Desert Cat

The caracal is a slender, muscular cat with long legs that lives in the Negev Desert, in other areas of the Middle East, and in Africa. Adult males can weigh up to 40 pounds (18 kilograms), and females up to about 24 pounds (11 kg). The caracal hunts at night, feasting on rodents, rabbits, and birds. Caracals are extremely skilled jumpers and can catch birds in flight, often more than one at a time. Occasionally, the caracal preys on larger animals such as small antelopes or ostriches.

Numerous endangered bird species, including several types of vultures and white-tailed sea eagles, are bred in captivity and released into the wild to prevent extinction.

Reptiles and Amphibians

Israel has ninety-seven different species of reptiles, including forty varieties of snakes. The poisonous Persian horned viper lives in the desert and is one of the few poisonous species of snake in Israel. The prehistoric-looking Egyptian mastigure, which can grow to 2.5 feet (76 cm) long, lives in the Arava region, where it feeds on bugs and acacia trees. Geckos and chameleons are found throughout the country.

Symbols of the Nation

Israel's national animal is a small antelope called the Israeli gazelle. It feeds on plants, bushes, and grass. Until the 1950s, its population was steadily decreasing. Its population was in decline because it was being hunted by both humans and the Iranian wolf. Since that time, conservation efforts have restored the number of Israeli gazelles. The gazelles live predominantly in the Golan Heights and the Galilee.

In 2008, the people of Israel chose the hoopoe as the country's national bird. The colorful hoopoe measures about 10 to 12.5 inches (25 to 32 cm) long. It feeds mostly on insects, such as beetles, locusts, and crickets. Occasionally, its habit of feeding on things within the soil turns up delicacies such as small reptiles and frogs. The hoopoe's name comes from the unique "oop-oop-oop" song it makes when calling.

The most common amphibian in Israel is the European green toad. It lives along the Mediterranean shore. Israel's smallest amphibian is Savigny's tree frog, which grows to only 1.5 inches (4 cm) long. It lives around plants and trees, and can change its color to adapt to different shades of green in its environment.

Israel is also home to several types of land tortoise, including the Mediterranean spur-thighed tortoise and the Egyptian tortoise, a desert dweller. Although the Mediterranean tortoise was one of the first wildlife species to be protected by government regulations, it has disappeared from some parts of Israel. It is now a popular pet.

Green toads can live anywhere from cities to mountains to semideserts.

Sea Life

Many varieties of fish live in Israel's seas and inland waters. The Mediterranean coast is inhabited by bass, mullet, sharks, and many types of shellfish. Israel's most prized fish habitat is the coral reef near Eilat on the Gulf of Aqaba. The reef stretches 1.5 miles (2.4 km) along the shoreline. It is home to 1,270 species of fish, 1,120 species of shellfish, and hundreds of varieties of coral. Whale sharks, dolphins, and dugongs make the reef's mazes and deep canyons their homes. The beach area serves as a nesting ground for hawksbill sea turtles. At the Underwater Observatory Marine Park at Eilat, visitors can view life in the reef from beneath sea level, in the comfort of an underwater observatory.

The hawksbill sea turtle gets its name from its curved mouth. Its beaklike mouth enables it to reach into holes and cracks to find food.

Protecting Nature

The Israeli government takes care to protect the country's diverse landscapes, plant and animal life, and national parks and reserves. The Israel Nature and Parks Authority (INPA) works to protect ecosystems and landscapes throughout Israel. By 2007, the INPA oversaw 190 nature reserves and 66 national parks, covering about 20 percent of Israel's land area.

The INPA runs breeding centers to reintroduce wildlife species that have become extinct. To date, the INPA has reintroduced ostriches and fallow deer, Arabian oryx (large antelopes), and onagers (short-legged relatives of the horse, above). The INPA has about two hundred additional nature reserves and national parks in various stages of being declared protected areas.

Remembering a Turbulent Past

ACCORDING TO TRADITIONAL JUDEO-CHRISTIAN beliefs, which are based on the Bible, the history of the Jewish people begins roughly five thousand years ago. Around 3000 BCE, groups of peoples known as the Canaanites lived in the region of present-day Israel. In about 1800 BCE, Semitic peoples from Mesopotamia in southwestern Asia, north of modern Israel, moved to Canaan (Palestine's biblical name). These were the ancient Hebrews. The Hebrews, also known as the Israelites, lived in the region of the Nile River delta, where they were enslaved by the Egyptians.

Around 1300 BCE, the Israelites escaped Egypt and eventually returned to Canaan. Israelite king David established Jerusalem as the capital. Following David's death, his son Solomon built the First Temple of Jerusalem, where the Israelites worshipped their god. After Solomon's death, the Israelites split their kingdom into two parts: the northern part was called Israel, with its capital at Samaria; the southern part, with Jerusalem as its capital, was called Judah. The people in the south were known as the Jewish people.

Opposite: **David is crowned king of Judah. According to Jewish tradition, David became king in about 1010 BCE.**

Israel's Archaeological Treasures

Israel is one of the world's most explored lands, with hundreds of digs and archaeological expeditions made annually. Thousands of uncovered sites have opened the window to the region's rich history and culture through the centuries.

Digs at the Carmel Caves, south of Haifa, have unearthed 250,000-year-old stone tools and blades, and animal bones. Scientists believe these to be the trash of the human prehistoric dwellers. The artifacts may be evidence of the earliest-known people to live on earth.

Ashkelon sits on Israel's Mediterranean coast. In the course of its nearly ten-thousand-year-old history, Canaanites, Philistines, Israelites, Babylonians, Greeks, Romans, Egyptians, and Christian crusaders inhabited Ashkelon. It was once an important ancient seaport. Recent digs at Ashkelon have revealed fortifications, a large gate to the city, and one hundred skeletons.

Tel Megiddo (above), overlooking the Jezreel Valley in the north, is one of the most important cities from biblical times. It was inhabited as early as nine thousand years ago, and archaeologists have uncovered horse stables, an altar, grain pits, a large Greek floor mosaic, and a third-century Christian church.

One of the world's most important archaeological finds was made in 1947 by a young shepherd exploring caves in Qumran, along the western shore of the Dead Sea. Muhammad adh-Dhib found jars that contained parchment scrolls wrapped in linen. The documents, now known as the Dead Sea Scrolls, were written by ancient Jews in the first century BCE. Later digs unearthed more scrolls and fragments in nearby caves. The scrolls, written in Hebrew and Aramaic, contain biblical texts and descriptions of daily life. They reveal a history of ancient Jewish life and religious thought. Today, the scrolls are on display at the Israel Museum in Jerusalem.

Foreign Invaders

In the following centuries, the two kingdoms came under constant attack from others in the region. In 722 BCE, the Assyrians conquered Israel. The Babylonians then conquered the Assyrians. Around 597 BCE, the Babylonians conquered Judah and destroyed the First Temple. The Jews were exiled to Babylon as slaves. In 539 BCE, the Persians defeated the Babylonians and allowed the Jews to return to Jerusalem. The Jews built the Second Temple, reestablishing their center of religious worship.

The Assyrians captured Samaria, a fortress city in Israel, in the eighth century BCE.

In 332 BCE, Alexander the Great of Macedonia, a kingdom north of Greece, conquered the entire region. The Egyptians and the Seleucids, from Syria, later gained control of the area. Seleucid ruler Antiochus IV outlawed the Jewish religion, which led to a bloody uprising that ultimately resulted in Jewish independence in 141 BCE.

But independence was short-lived. In 63 BCE, the Romans took control of Judah and renamed the land Judea. In 66 CE, the Jews launched the Great Revolt against the Romans. In retaliation, four years later the Romans destroyed the Second Temple, leaving only one wall standing. In 135, the Romans crushed yet another Jewish rebellion, led by Simon Bar-Kokhba. The Romans destroyed Jerusalem and drove the Jews from the city.

The Jews fled to the Greek Islands, the Black Sea, the coasts of the Mediterranean, and northern and eastern Europe. This scattering of the Jews to other lands became known as the Diaspora. As an insult to the banished Jews, the Romans renamed the province of Judea, calling it Palestine, after the Philistines, who were remembered as one of the Jews' ancient enemies.

The Fate of Palestine

The Romans ruled Palestine for the next five hundred years. During that time, Christianity developed a strong presence in the region and throughout the Roman Empire. After three hundred years of bitter persecution by the Romans, Christianity became the empire's official religion in 313.

The Fortress of Masada

On the eastern fringe of the Judean Desert overlooking the Dead Sea, the ancient fortress of Masada sits high atop a steep-edged plateau. Built by Roman king Herod the Great from 37 to 31 BCE, the complex included a palace, defense towers, soldiers' barracks, and an armory.

In 66 CE, Jewish rebels gained control of Masada and used the fortress as a refuge from the Romans. For six years, the rebels lived on Masada, using it as a base from which to harass local Roman armies. In 72, a force of 15,000 Romans laid siege to Masada. Rather than be destroyed by the Romans, the rebels inside the fortress set fire to their storerooms of food and committed mass suicide. According to an account of the time, 960 Jewish people—men, women, and children—perished.

Many of the ancient buildings at Masada have been restored, including the synagogue that the rebels built in which to worship during their years occupying the fortress. Today, Masada is viewed as a symbol of the bravery and heroism of early Jews in their quest for freedom.

The Western Wall

The only structure the Romans left standing when they destroyed the Second Temple was a 187-foot-tall (57 m), 1,600-foot-long (500 m) outer wall surrounding the Temple Mount. This remaining piece of the most sacred building in the Jewish world rapidly became the holiest location in Jewish life. For almost two thousand years, Jews have come to pray at the wall, often slipping written prayer notes into its cracks.

The wall is a gathering place for Friday night religious services and all Jewish holidays, particularly on the fast of Tisha B'Av, which remembers the destruction of the First and Second Temples.

There were several surviving Jewish communities in Palestine, but most of the people living there were Christian.

Around 570, the Prophet Muhammad was born in Mecca, in what is now Saudi Arabia. Muhammad would grow up to preach about a new religion, called Islam. Like Christianity, Islam quickly took root in the region. Believers in Islam are called Muslims.

When the Roman Empire fell in 476, the Byzantines took control of the region. In 638, Muslim armies attacked the Byzantines and gained control of Jerusalem. The city was recaptured by Christian crusaders from Europe in 1099, but it fell back into Muslim control in 1187 under an army led by Saladin. After Saladin died, the Christians regained Jerusalem, but in 1291, Muslims finally forced the crusaders out of Palestine. Many Jews, who had left the region during these troubled and violent times, returned to their homeland. In 1517, the Ottoman Empire, which was based in Turkey, ousted the Muslim Egyptian Mamluks who controlled Palestine. The Ottomans allowed the Jewish community to grow. For the next three hundred years, Jews from Europe and eastern Asia flocked to Palestine.

Zionism

In the late 1800s, a Jewish social and political movement called Zionism was born. The movement took its name from the word *Zion*, a biblical name for Jerusalem. Zionism was a

Christian crusaders seized Jerusalem from its Muslim rulers in 1099. Experts estimate that about thirty-seven thousand men took part in this crusade.

Chaim Weizmann was a chemist and college professor who became a leader in the Zionist movement. In 1949, he became the first president of Israel.

response to the waves of anti-Semitism (hostility against Jews) in Europe. Zionists wanted a Jewish state to be established in Palestine, roughly on the site of ancient Israel, as a place where Jews from all over the world could come and live without fear of persecution by others.

Led by people such as Theodor Herzl and Chaim Weizmann, the movement gained popularity. Tens of thousands of Jews immigrated to Palestine. They bought land, established farming communities, and later founded the city of Tel Aviv. Although tensions ran high between the Arab residents of Palestine and the new Jewish immigrants, the flood of newcomers continued. By 1914, about 85,000 of Palestine's 615,000 inhabitants were Jewish. The rest were mostly Arabs.

Palestine During the World Wars

World War I (1914–1918) pitted Great Britain, France, Russia, and later the United States (together called the Allies) against Germany, Austria-Hungary, and the Ottoman Empire. The Allies agreed to divide the lands of the Ottoman Empire if they won the war. To weaken the Ottomans, the British promised support for a Jewish state if the Jews of Germany and the Ottoman Empire fought on the side of the Allies. In November

Theodor Herzl

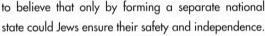

One of the leading voices of the Zionist movement was Theodor Herzl (1860–1904). Herzl was a Hungarian-born Jew who studied law and then became a journalist. He originally believed that the way to end European anti-Semitism was for Jews living there to integrate with Christian societies. Eventually, he came to believe that only by forming a separate national state could Jews ensure their safety and independence.

His pamphlet, *Der Judenstaat* (*The Jewish State*), published in 1896, argued for the establishment of a Jewish homeland. Herzl called upon other nations to recognize the Zionist movement. In 1897, he organized the first Zionist Congress, which was held in Basel, Switzerland. There, Palestine, which was then part of the Ottoman Empire, was chosen as the home of a possible future Jewish state. The congress founded the World Zionist Organization to provide economic support for the new state. Herzl became its first president.

Herzl's initial attempts to convince the Ottomans to allow Jews to settle in Palestine, and to rally international support for a Jewish state, met with little success. However, his energy and tireless efforts ultimately helped make Zionism a powerful political force, which resulted in the establishment of a Jewish homeland forty-four years after his death.

1917, the British government issued the Balfour Declaration, which promised to establish a homeland for the Jews in Palestine after the war. The British, however, also promised land to the Arabs to establish their own state in return for their support. Neither promise clearly defined the borders of the proposed new states. This error was to have deadly consequences in the years to follow. The British remained in control of Palestine until 1948.

The Allies won the war, and tens of thousands of Jews immigrated to Palestine, confident that a homeland would soon be created. Many of the new arrivals during the 1930s were fleeing Nazi persecution in Germany and Poland. Led by Adolf Hitler, the Nazis seized Jewish property and did not allow Jews to vote or own businesses. Meanwhile, Arab anti-Jewish violence in Palestine increased. In 1936, a violent revolt by Palestinian Arabs against Jews and British authorities broke out. The Arabs demanded an end to both Jewish immigration and future land sales to Jews. Most importantly, the Arabs called for an Arab state in Palestine. The British responded favorably to the Arab requests. In 1933 and again in 1936, they set sharp restrictions on Jewish immigration to Palestine.

Adolf Hitler promoted anti-Semitism during his rise to power in Germany.

With the start of World War II (1939–1945), the Palestinian issue was temporarily left to simmer. In this conflict, the Axis powers of Germany, Japan, and Italy fought the Allies, which included Britain, France, and later the United States and the Soviet Union. The war claimed the lives of more than seventy million people worldwide. In Europe, the Nazis murdered six million Jews, or about two-thirds of all the Jews living there. The catastrophe became known as the Holocaust. Responding to the tragedy, many people, Jews and non-Jews, rallied to support the Zionist cause. Meanwhile, tens of thousands of homeless Jewish war survivors living in refugee camps in Europe were denied entry to Palestine by the British government.

The Nazis rounded up Jews from around Europe and shipped them to concentration camps. More than three million Jews were killed in the camps.

With the conclusion of the war, attention was again focused on the fate of Palestine. Weary of the constant violence, Britain turned over the matter to the newly created United Nations (UN), an international organization dedicated to solving conflicts peacefully. In November 1947, the UN decided Palestine should be divided into two separate states, one Jewish and one Arab. A map of the divided land was drawn up. The Jews accepted the plan, but the Arabs did not.

Finally, on May 14, 1948, the day before Britain was to give up its claim to Palestine, Jewish leaders declared the birth of

In 1947, representatives at the United Nations discussed the division of Palestine.

their new state, Israel. The next day, military forces from Lebanon, Jordan, Egypt, Syria, and Iraq attacked the new nation. The conflict would become known as the War of Independence. Israel defeated its attackers and gained 50 percent of the land that the UN had given the Palestinian Arabs. A peace treaty was signed in January 1949.

In the first Israeli elections, Chaim Weizmann was elected president, and David Ben-Gurion was elected prime minister. During the 1950s, the young nation grew as industry, farming, and new cities and towns rapidly developed.

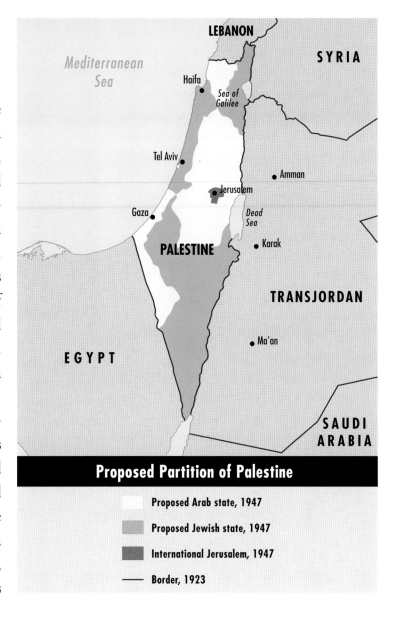

Proposed Partition of Palestine

☐ Proposed Arab state, 1947

▨ Proposed Jewish state, 1947

▦ International Jerusalem, 1947

—— Border, 1923

Peace, however, was short-lived. In 1956, Israel attacked Egypt for taking control of the Suez Canal. The canal was located within Egypt, but it was partly owned by the French and British. Israel took control of Egypt's Sinai Peninsula and the Gaza Strip but pulled back its troops after the war ended. Arab-Israeli clashes continued throughout the 1960s, leading

The First Prime Minister

David Ben-Gurion (1886–1973) is often considered the founder of Israel. Ben-Gurion was born in Poland in 1886. He became a strong supporter of the Zionist movement. In 1912, he moved to Palestine, but the Ottoman authorities forced him to leave because of his political activities. He settled in New York City in 1915, and in 1918, he joined the British army and fought in World War I. Following the war, Ben-Gurion returned to Palestine, which was then under British control. In 1935, he was elected head of the World Zionist Organization and the Jewish Agency for Palestine, becoming the leading figure in the effort for Jews to secure a homeland in the region.

In 1948, Ben-Gurion supervised the nation's military operations in the War of Independence, which began the day after he announced the creation of the new and independent nation of Israel. The Israelis

defeated the five Arab nations—Iraq, Syria, Egypt, Jordan, and Lebanon—that had invaded the new state. Following Israel's victory, Ben-Gurion was elected Israel's first prime minister. He served as prime minster from 1948 to 1953 and 1955 to 1963, effectively leading the new nation through its tumultuous early years.

to the Six-Day War fought in June 1967. Israel attacked Syria, Egypt, and Jordan, and defeated them in less than one week. Israel recaptured the Sinai and the Gaza Strip, and took control of the Golan Heights from Syria, and the West Bank and East Jerusalem from Jordan. About one million Palestinian Arabs lived in the newly occupied territories at that time.

In the aftermath of Israel's victory, the Palestinian Liberation Organization (PLO), which had formed in 1964, increased its attacks on Israeli military and civilian targets. The PLO was led by Yasser Arafat (1929–2004), a Palestinian born in France. Its goal was to establish a Palestinian homeland

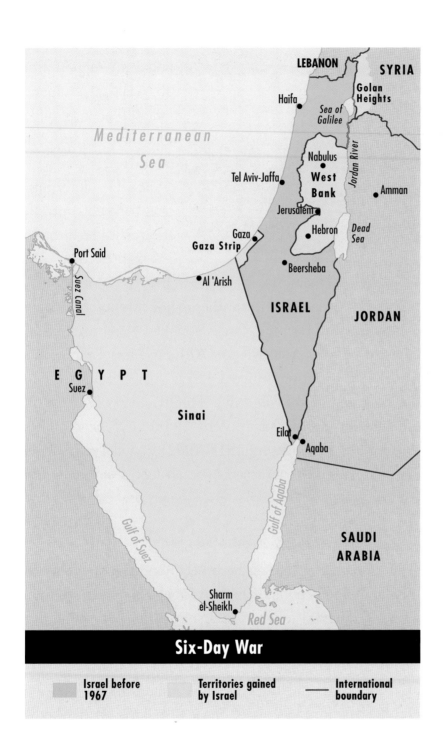

LEBANON

SYRIA

Golan
Heights

Haifa

*Sea of
Galilee*

Mediterranean

Sea

Jordan River

Nabulus

Tel Aviv-Jaffa

**West
Bank**

Amman

Jerusalem

Gaza

Hebron

*Dead
Sea*

Gaza Strip

Beersheba

ISRAEL

JORDAN

Port Said

Suez Canal

Al 'Arish

E G Y P T

Suez

Sinai

Eilat

Aqaba

Gulf of Aqaba

Gulf of Suez

**SAUDI
ARABIA**

Sharm
el-Sheikh

Red Sea

Six-Day War

Israel before 1967	**Territories gained by Israel**	**International boundary**

Israel's well-trained air force helped it win the Six-Day War.

and gain support from all Arab governments. Israel frequently raided PLO centers in Arab countries.

Israel's determination to keep control of the territories acquired in the Six-Day War and to control all of Jerusalem eventually led to another major conflict. In October 1973, Syrian and Egyptian forces attacked Israel on the holiest Jewish holiday, Yom Kippur. Although Israel retained its territories, the nation suffered heavy losses. Minor clashes followed the October fighting. Finally, in 1979, Egyptian president Anwar el-Sadat (1918–1981) and Israeli prime minister Menachem Begin (1913–1992) signed a peace agreement. Over the next four years, Israeli forces withdrew from the Sinai.

Intifada

In 1982, Israel attacked southern Lebanon in response to PLO attacks that had been launched on Israel from positions there. Fighting continued for three years, until the UN came in to replace Israeli troops in Lebanon.

In 1987, violent protests by Arabs against the Israeli occupation in Gaza and the West Bank erupted. This campaign was called the intifada, which means "shaking off" in Arabic.

Many people were killed. The United States urged Israel to settle its conflict with the PLO. In 1993, Arafat and Israeli prime minister Yitzhak Rabin (1922–1995) exchanged letters in which Israel recognized the PLO, and the PLO denounced violence. This laid the foundation for later talks aimed at a settlement in which Israel would withdraw from Gaza and the West Bank, and Arabs living in those regions would be allowed to govern themselves.

In 1994, the Israelis signed a peace treaty with Jordan and entered into peace negotiations with Syria, a longtime

U.S. president Bill Clinton (center) brokered the peace accords between Israeli prime minister Yitzhak Rabin (right) and King Hussein of Jordan (left).

supporter of the Palestinian cause. These positive signs signaled hope for peace in the region. Rabin was assassinated in 1995 by an Israeli extremist who disagreed with Rabin's efforts to negotiate this particular peace agreement.

An Uncertain Peace

Violence continued in the early 2000s. A second intifada began in September 2000 in Israel and in Palestinian territories. In 2005, Israel and the moderate Palestinian leadership

Palestinian Territories

Since 1996, the Palestinian Authority (PA) has been responsible for civil government in Gaza and the West Bank, lands occupied by Israel starting in 1967. However, Israel still holds military control of both the West Bank and Gaza. In 2005, Israel removed nine thousand Jewish settlers and its last remaining soldiers from Gaza. Thus, while Israel controls the borders of the Gaza Strip, it is not directly involved in governing it. The following year, members of the Hamas militant political party won control of the PA. Hamas now controls political policy in the Gaza Strip and sometimes shoots rockets across the border into Israel, most of which fall on civilian areas.

The PA currently has full or shared control of about 40 percent of the West Bank, west of the Jordan River. Palestinians are seeking full control of the entire West Bank, including areas along the Jordan River and East Jerusalem, which they would like to make

the capital of a Palestinian state. The Israeli government considers all of Jerusalem to be one city and the capital of Israel. Thus, the status of East Jerusalem remains an unresolved issue in this conflict. Despite many attempts to hammer out a peaceful solution to the Israeli-Palestinian conflict, little progress has been made in recent years.

agreed to a cease-fire. Prime Minister Ariel Sharon pulled all Israeli residents and troops out of Gaza.

In 2006, the situation flared up again. Israel attacked a militant group called Hezbollah in Lebanon after two Israeli soldiers were kidnapped. About 1,000 Lebanese and 150 Israelis died in the conflict. Then, in late 2008 and early 2009, Israel responded to rocket fire from the Gaza Strip with a series of air strikes and a ground invasion. More than a thousand Palestinians died and tens of thousands were left homeless.

In 2011, diplomats from the United States took steps to bring Israelis and Palestinians to the bargaining table, in the hopes of negotiating a peace agreement. Only time will tell if their efforts will get the peace process back on track.

Ariel Sharon served as a general in the Israel Defense Forces before entering politics.

Governing a Nation

On May 14, 1948, Zionist leaders issued a declaration of independence for the new state of Israel. The Declaration of the Establishment of the State of Israel noted the religious and spiritual connection of the Jewish people to Israel. It claimed that the new nation would be "based on freedom, justice, and peace," and it appealed to the United Nations and Jews around the world to assist the development of the young state. It also asked the Arab residents of Israel to work for peace and to participate in building the new nation. While Jews around the world rejoiced, the Arab world reacted negatively to the establishment of a Jewish state in Palestine. On May 15, troops from five Arab nations attacked Israel. The fighting lasted eight months and cost the lives of four thousand Israeli soldiers, two thousand Israeli civilians, and between eight thousand and fifteen thousand Arabs. Hundreds of thousands of Arabs fled Palestine, becoming refugees in the war-torn region. Arabs refer to May 15 as "the catastrophe."

Opposite: **Girls dance at an Independence Day celebration.**

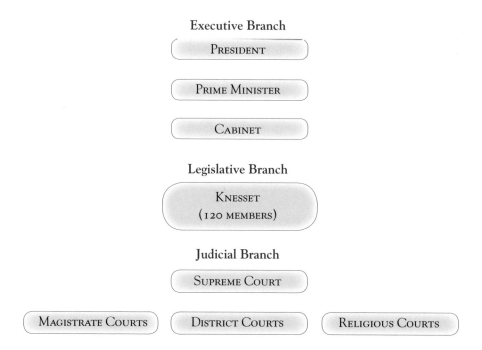

National Government of Israel

Executive Branch

PRESIDENT

PRIME MINISTER

CABINET

Legislative Branch

KNESSET
(120 MEMBERS)

Judicial Branch

SUPREME COURT

MAGISTRATE COURTS   DISTRICT COURTS   RELIGIOUS COURTS

The Government of Israel

Israel is a parliamentary democracy. It has a head of state called the president, a prime minister, a one-house legislature called the Knesset, and a judicial branch made up of several different court systems.

The president is elected to a single, seven-year term by the Knesset. The president's role is primarily ceremonial, much like the king or queen of Great Britain. The president nominates a prime minister and signs treaties and laws approved by the Knesset. He or she also appoints judges, ambassadors, and the governor of the Bank of Israel. According to law, the president may "neither intervene politically nor express personal views on issues that divide the public."

The Israeli Flag

The national flag of Israel features a six-pointed blue Star of David on a white background centered between two horizontal blue bands. This was the flag of the Zionist movement, which had adopted the design at the First Zionist Congress in 1897. It was officially adopted as the flag of the State of Israel on October 28, 1948.

The Star of David began to be widely used in the nineteenth century on Jewish religious objects and in synagogues throughout Europe. The star became the symbol of the Zionist movement, although it had no particular religious significance. In time, the star came to signify Judaism to both Jews and non-Jews alike. The

two blue stripes on the Israeli flag were inspired by the blue stripes on the tallith, the traditional prayer shawl worn by Jewish men during religious ceremonies.

The prime minister is the head of the government and the most powerful figure in Israeli politics. He or she is elected by the Knesset to a four-year term. The prime minister heads the cabinet, the policymaking body in Israel, and appoints cabinet members. The cabinet has thirty members, each overseeing a specific area of policy, including finance, health, education, national defense, tourism, and many others.

The Knesset is the Israeli government's lawmaking body. The Knesset elects the prime minister and president. It also enacts laws; approves the budget, taxes, and members of the cabinet; and oversees the work of the government. The Knesset has 120 members, who are elected to four-year terms. While most members of the Knesset are Jewish, dozens of Arabs have served in the Knesset over the years, usually constituting around 10 percent of the total membership.

The National Anthem

"Hatikvah" ("The Hope") is the national anthem of Israel. It is a poem written by Ukrainian Naphtali Herz Imber in 1878. Imber's poem was a tribute to the hopes of Petah Tikva, one of the first Jewish settlements in Ottoman-controlled Palestine. Samuel Cohen provided the music, based on a common European folk tune, in 1888. "Hatikvah" was adopted as Israel's unofficial anthem in 1948, but it wasn't until 2004 that it became the official anthem.

Hebrew lyrics

Kol'od balleivav penimah
Nefesh yehudi homiyah,
Ul(e)fa'atei mizrach kadimah,
'Ayin letziyon tzofiyah;
'Od lo avdah tikvateinu,
Hatikvah bat shnot alpayim,
Lihyot 'am chofshi be'artzeinu,
Eretz-tziyon (v)'Y(e)rushalayim.

English translation

As long as in the heart, within,
A Jewish soul still yearns,
And onward, towards the ends of the east,
An eye still gazes toward Zion;
Our hope is not yet lost,
The hope of two thousand years,
To be a free people in our land,
The land of Zion and Jerusalem.

The judicial branch of government includes the Supreme Court and several lower courts. The Supreme Court has the final word in all judicial matters in Israel and in Israeli-occupied territories. Usually, twelve judges sit on the court, but the number can vary. The president appoints Supreme Court judges, whose terms end when they reach seventy years of age. The judicial system incorporates criminal, civil, and military courts. Separate religious courts for Jews, Muslims, Christians, and Druze handle cases of marriage, divorce, and inheritance.

Serving in the Army

Israeli citizens over the age of eighteen must serve in the Israel Defense Forces (IDF), although Arab and Druze citizens are exempt. Exemptions are also made for those who are handicapped or who have religious objections to serving. Men serve

Golda Meir

Golda Meir (1898–1978) has been Israel's only woman prime minister, serving from 1969 to 1974. Meir was born in Kiev, Russia, and moved to Milwaukee, Wisconsin, in 1906. In 1921, she emigrated to Palestine, where she was active in the growing Zionist movement during the 1930s and 1940s. Meir was Israel's minister of foreign affairs from 1956 to 1966. Three years later, she was elected prime minister. During her term in office, Meir worked steadily for a peace settlement in the Middle East. She resigned her position in 1974 following widespread criticism that Israel had been unprepared for the Yom Kippur War of 1973.

An Israeli soldier on duty in the Gaza Strip. About 187,000 people are on active duty in the Israel Defense Forces.

three years, and women serve two. Women who volunteer for combat positions may be required to serve three years because of longer training periods. Israel is the only nation that drafts women and places some of them in combat service.

Students may request to attend college or university before serving in the IDF. If approved, the cost of their bachelor's degree is paid by the army, although students must agree to extend their army service by two or three years.

The IDF sometimes requires men to serve in reserve service for up to one month a year, until the age of forty-five. Active reserve duty can be imposed in times of national crisis.

Soldiers can continue to serve in the army after their regular service, for a short or long period of time. This is called permanent service.

Jerusalem

Israel's capital and largest city, Jerusalem is often regarded as the world's holiest city. It is the spiritual hub for three religions: Judaism, Christianity, and Islam.

Jerusalem is located in the Judean Hills and the West Bank. The city is made of three main areas: the old city, West Jerusalem, and East Jerusalem. The old city is divided into four quarters—Jewish, Christian, Muslim, and Orthodox Christian, or Armenian. A maze of narrow alleys connects the four quarters and the many religious sites found in each one. The major sites include the Western Wall, Islam's Dome of the Rock and the al-Aqsa Mosque, and the Church of the Holy Sepulchre, Christianity's holiest site. West Jerusalem, also known as the new city, is the city's governmental and commercial center. East Jerusalem is the older part of the city and home to a large Arab population.

Since 1967, the population of Jerusalem has more than doubled to 773,700. Of the total, 64 percent are Jewish, 32 percent are Muslim, and 2 percent are Christian. The largest percentage increase has occurred in the Arab population. To maintain a Jewish majority and protect a Jewish claim to the city, the Israeli government has encouraged Jews to settle in Jerusalem. Many Jews have since moved into the traditionally Arab East Jerusalem, and settlements have been built to house the newcomers. The government's efforts to ensure that Jerusalem's population will be more Jewish has been accompanied by conflict and controversy.

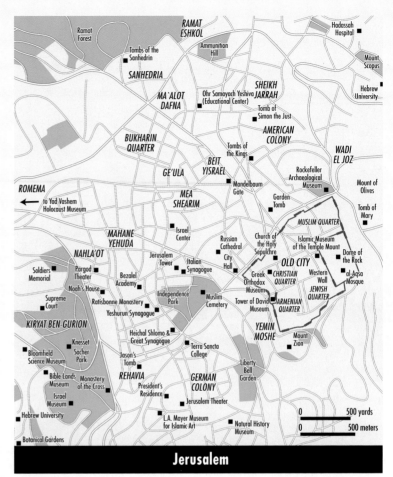

Jerusalem

Modern Jerusalem is a bustling metropolis of shopping malls, luxury hotels, and offices and factories. The Knesset, Israel's parliament, is located near the city center, as is the Israel Museum. The Islamic Museum in the old city displays world-class collections of coins, ceramics, and military items. In West Jerusalem, Yad Vashem (the Holocaust Museum) memorializes the six million Jews killed by German Nazis during World War II. Other sites of note in Jerusalem are the Hebrew University and the eleventh-century Monastery of the Cross, currently occupied by monks of the Greek Orthodox Church of Jerusalem.

A Busy
Economy

A T THE TIME OF ITS DECLARATION OF INDEPENDENCE in 1948, Israel faced an uncertain economic future. With limited natural resources and an undeveloped farming and industrial base, the country was relatively poor. Tens of thousands of immigrants were pouring into the country, but Israel lacked basic public services for the new arrivals. The near-constant threat from neighboring Arab nations at first diverted the government's attention to protecting the new state, rather than building a stable economy.

But hard work and a nationwide commitment by the Israelis to develop their land began paying off in the 1950s. The economy began to boom. Today, about 82 percent of the Israeli labor force have service jobs. These include positions in government, health, education, tourism, and the financial sector.

About 16 percent of the workers are in industry, which includes manufacturing and mining. Israel's high-technology industries, including aviation, computers, and electronics, have become

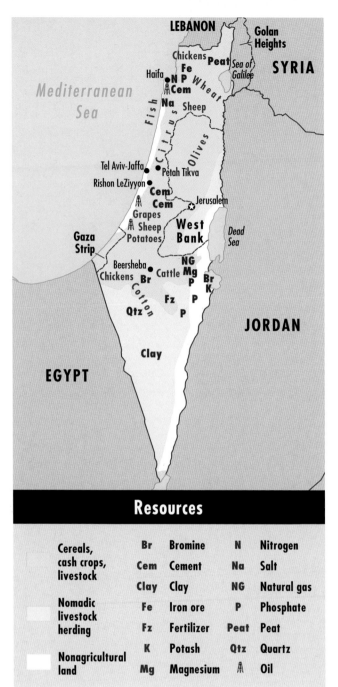

Resources

Cereals, cash crops, livestock	Br	Bromine	N	Nitrogen
	Cem	Cement	Na	Salt
	Clay	Clay	NG	Natural gas
Nomadic livestock herding	Fe	Iron ore	P	Phosphate
	Fz	Fertilizer	Peat	Peat
	K	Potash	Qtz	Quartz
Nonagricultural land	Mg	Magnesium	⚒	Oil

the nation's most-developed sectors, many continuing to grow quickly. Two percent of the labor force works in agriculture.

Farming

Hardworking Israelis turned what was once desert, swamp, and poor, rocky soil into productive farmlands. Swamps were drained, rocks were removed, and innovative irrigation technologies were brought to the desert. Barren soil became rich, fertile fields. Israel produces about 95 percent of its own food needs.

Israel is a leading producer and exporter of citrus fruits, avocados, mangoes, and guava. These crops grow well in orchards on Israel's Mediterranean coast. During the winter, several varieties of melon are grown in the valleys. In drier regions, bananas and dates are harvested. In the northern hill region, apples, pears, blueberries, and cherries are grown. The Golan also produces field crops, such as corn, tomatoes, onions, and cotton. Grape vineyards can be found throughout the country.

One reason for Israel's successful agricultural production is the creative use and conservation of water. Israel's average annual rainfall varies from 35 inches (89 cm) in the north to only 1.2 inches (3 cm) in the south. The problem of a lack of water was solved in the 1960s, when the National Water Carrier system was created. A complex system of pumping stations, pipes, tunnels, dams, and reservoirs was developed to bring water from the northern regions to the south. Israeli scientists invented a technique called drip irrigation to conserve water and make irrigation more efficient. In this technique,

The National Water Carrier system is about 80 miles (130 km) long. It carries water from the Sea of Galilee to dry areas of the south.

What Israel Grows, Makes, and Mines

Agriculture (2009)

Potatoes	608,832 metric tons
Tomatoes	454,761 metric tons
Chicken meat	436,000 metric tons

Manufacturing (value added, 2006)

Medicines and soaps	US$2,585,000,000
Medical, measuring, and testing equipment	US$2,502,000,000
Electronics	US$2,336,000,000

Mining (2008)

Potash	2,300,000 metric tons
Bromine	164,000 metric tons
Magnesium metal	35,000 metric tons

water is carried through a network of pipes with small feeder holes that run above the crops. The right amount of water is dripped directly onto each plant's roots. Drip irrigation saves water, which is wasted by traditional sprinkler systems.

Industry

Chemical and medical products, high-tech electronics, diamond cutting and polishing, and textile and apparel manufacturing rank among Israel's most important industries. Many of the chemical plants are located near Haifa Bay and the Dead Sea. Teva Pharmaceutical Industries is one of the largest generic drug companies in the world.

Although diamonds are not mined in Israel, they are imported and then cut and polished into fine gems, industrial drill bits, and cutting tools. Israel is a center of diamond cutting, along with India and Belgium.

Israeli computer engineering companies excel in fields from robotics to communications. Military engineers have produced breakthroughs in air defense systems, tanks, weapons,

A jeweler in Tel Aviv evaluates a diamond.

and satellites. Genetic scientists in Israel have discovered new techniques for battling disease. They have also invented equipment such as surgical lasers, scanners, and medical cameras to diagnose and treat illness.

The Weizmann Institute of Science in Rehovot is one of the world's leading research centers in computer science, biology, physics, chemistry, and math. Graduates of the school often go on to work for major Israeli high-tech companies.

Solar panels, which turn sunlight into electricity, cover the roof of a building at the Weizmann Institute of Science.

Israeli Currency

Israel's official currency is the new shekel. In 2011, 3.39 new shekalim equaled one U.S. dollar. The new shekel is divided into 100 agorot (the singular is agora).

Coins have values of 1 agora; 5 and 10 agorot; 1 new shekel; and 2, 5, and 10 new shekalim. Paper money comes in values of 20, 50, 100, and 200 shekalim. The 50-shekalim note has a picture of author Shmuel Yosef Agnon on the front; on the reverse are images of Jerusalem, the Temple Mount, and Agnon's notebooks, pen, and glasses.

Tourism

Tourism is a leading industry in Israel, bringing in more than $3.3 billion annually. About 2.7 million people visit Israel every year. Most tourists are from the United States, Russia, Germany, France, and Great Britain. About 54 percent of the visitors are Christian and 39 percent are Jewish.

Jerusalem and Tel Aviv are the most-visited cities in Israel. As a holy city of Judaism, Christianity, and Islam, Jerusalem offers tourists many religious and historical sites. Tel Aviv's bustling street life appeals to many visitors. Scenic hiking trails throughout Israel allow visitors to explore the country on foot. The Gulf of Aqaba, the Mediterranean coastal strip, and the Dead Sea offer sunny beaches and first-rate resorts. Skiers enjoy the slopes of Mount Hermon in the Golan Heights, while divers can explore the coral reefs off the shores of the Gulf of Aqaba.

The streets of Tel Aviv are often jammed with cars.

Transportation

Israel has a well-developed transportation system, which includes a large network of paved roads and bus, train, and airline services. There are 11,360 miles (18,290 km) of paved roads and highways spanning the country. There are about 2.5 million cars in Israel, with 239 cars per every 1,000 people, making Israel's roads some of the most congested in the world.

Israel has roughly 640 miles (1,000 km) of railroad track, serving mainly the west coast and central Israel. The busiest train line runs between Tel Aviv and Haifa. Railway use has sharply increased in recent years, with about 30 million riders in 2006, compared to only 2.5 million riders in 1990. Increased train usage helps ease congestion on the roadways. Buses are the most widely used form of public transportation. The Tel Aviv Central Bus Station is the country's largest terminal and the second-largest bus terminal in the world, after the Millennium Park Bus Depot in Delhi, India.

A light-rail system began operating in Jerusalem in 2011. This mass transit system will help people move about the busy city more easily.

Israel has forty-eight airports, with the largest being Ben-Gurion International Airport near Tel Aviv. The airport handles more than twelve million passengers each year. Haifa and Ashdod, on the Mediterranean coast, and Eilat, on the Gulf of Aqaba, are the largest ports in the country.

Communications

Regardless of where in Israel someone lives, it's easy to stay in touch with friends and family, business associates, and the outside world. There are more than 9 million cell phones in Israel and 3.3 million landlines. Israel's communication system is the most highly developed in the Middle East.

Nearly everyone in Israel has a cell phone.

The Israel Broadcasting Authority (IBA) is the national broadcasting network, and it operates two television channels, one in Hebrew and the other in Arabic. IBA also broadcasts on eight radio networks. About fifteen radio stations are privately owned.

Newspapers and magazines are eagerly read throughout Israel. Although most newspapers are in Hebrew, others are published in Arabic, German, French, English, Russian, Yiddish, Polish, and Hungarian. *Ma'ariv* (*Evening*), first published in 1948, and *Yediot Aharonot* (*Latest News*), which began in 1939, have the largest daily circulations of Hebrew newspapers. *Al Anba* (*The News*), published in Kuwait, is the major Arabic-language paper in Israel.

Many Israelis learn about current events from newspapers.

The Israelis

ROUGHLY 76 PERCENT OF ISRAELI CITIZENS ARE Jewish. Muslims, Christians, Druze, and others make up the rest of the population. Even prior to Israel's founding in 1948, Jews from around the world emigrated to Palestine. Since that time, hundreds of thousands of new arrivals have moved to Israel, establishing a diverse blend of traditions and cultures in the tiny nation.

Opposite: **Children gather at a bakery window in Jerusalem. About 28 percent of Israelis are under age fifteen.**

Immigration to Israel

In 1950, the newly established state of Israel formally abolished British restrictions on Jewish immigration into Palestine. The new policy, called the Law of Return, gave every Jew throughout the world the right to settle in Israel. In the first four months after independence was declared, 50,000 newcomers arrived in Israel. Many were survivors of the Holocaust in Europe. By 1951, 687,000 people had moved to Israel, almost half of them from Arab nations. Within three years, Israel had doubled its Jewish population.

Although many Jews came to Israel on their own, the Israeli government helped many others who faced danger in their home countries. Between 1948 and 1951, 50,000 Yemenite and 120,000 Iraqi Jews were airlifted out of their countries and brought to Israel. When famine devastated Ethiopia in 1984, 8,000 Jews living in refugee camps were evacuated to Israel. In the 1980s, 700,000 Jews were brought to Israel from the Soviet Union. In 1991, a military mission rescued Ethiopian Jews from an unstable political situation, bringing 14,500 people to Israel.

In 1991, Ethiopian Jews gathered in Addis Ababa, the capital of Ethiopia, before leaving for Israel.

Israeli Jews

Following the conquest of Jerusalem by the Romans, Jews scattered throughout the world in the event known as the Diaspora. They settled in new lands, adopting the culture, language, and customs of their neighbors. Yet many continued to practice and observe Judaism, following the laws and rituals of their religion. Centuries later, the descendants of these people returned to Israel, bringing with them different languages, customs, and ways of practicing Judaism.

There are three main Jewish ethnic groups in Israel: the Ashkenazim, the Sephardim, and the Mizrahim. The Ashkenazim are mainly Jews of Russian and eastern and central European descent. They immigrated to Palestine in the late nineteenth and early twentieth centuries. Many Ashkenazim were leaders in the Zionist movement.

The Sephardim trace their heritage to Jews who were forced to leave Spain and Portugal in the late fifteenth century. Many settled in the Mediterranean countries of Greece, Turkey, Bulgaria, Italy, and North Africa. Others flocked

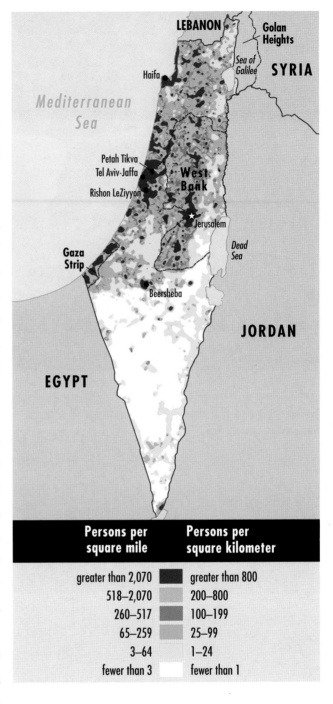

Persons per square mile	Persons per square kilometer
greater than 2,070	greater than 800
518–2,070	200–800
260–517	100–199
65–259	25–99
3–64	1–24
fewer than 3	fewer than 1

to South America and the Caribbean. A large number of Sephardim settled in Holland. The majority of immigrants to Israel after 1948 were Sephardim.

For several decades, tensions existed between Ashkenazi and Sephardic Jews. In the early years of statehood, the Sephardim were denied access to decision-making political positions. They were often viewed as culturally and intellectually inferior to the Ashkenazim. But in recent years, as the Sephardim have gained more political influence, the two groups have begun to close the gap between their economic and social differences.

Mizrahi Jews originated in the Islamic countries of North Africa and the Middle East. They steadily immigrated to Palestine for centuries, but the main waves of their immigration were in the 1950s, after Israel was established.

Israeli Arabs

Muslim Arabs are the second-largest ethnic group in Israel, making up about 20 percent of the population. About 75 to 80 percent of the Israeli Arab population is Muslim. Most of the Arab population lives in the northern and Haifa urban districts. Many Arabs work in construction and industry jobs.

As minorities in a land with a strong ethnic identity, Arabs suffer frequent discrimination. They are discriminated against in employment, housing, and land ownership. Proposals have been made in the Knesset to strip Arab Israelis of their citizenship. Yet Israel is committed to democratic ideals. Many Arabs

Ethnic Israel

Jewish	76%
Born in Israel	67%
Born in Europe and America	23%
Born in Africa	6%
Non-Jewish (mostly Arab)	24%

There are many Muslim Arabs in Jerusalem.

have served in the Knesset and in the military. Likewise, Israeli security forces have racially profiled Arabs, but in 2011, the Israeli Supreme Court ruled that this was illegal.

Bedouins

The Bedouin are an Arabic-speaking people. For centuries, they have lived in Middle Eastern deserts, ranging from western Africa to the Arabian Peninsula. An estimated 170,000 Bedouins live in Israel today, largely in the Negev Desert and desert areas in central and northern Israel. About forty different tribal groups make up the Bedouin population.

Many Bedouins continue to live a traditional nomadic lifestyle herding sheep, goats, and other livestock in the desert.

Bedouins were traditionally herders, and many still keep flocks of sheep and goats.

A woman serves tea in the Bedouin town of Rahat.

Using camels as their mode of transportation, they travel and trade along many of the same routes they have used for fifteen hundred years. They live in tents that they can quickly break down and set up when they move to a new spot.

In recent years, many Bedouins have settled in small towns and villages, some of which were built for them in the Negev by the Israeli government. Between 1979 and 1982, the Israeli government established seven Bedouin towns there. There are thirty-three elementary schools, three high schools, and three vocational schools in the Negev. Most of the students are boys because Bedouin society discourages the education of girls and women.

Population in major cities (2010 est.)

Jerusalem	773,700
Tel Aviv-Jaffa	403,700
Haifa	265,600
Rishon LeZiyyon	228,200
Petah Tikva	209,600

Resurrecting a Language

Until about 150 years ago, the Hebrew language was used only in prayers, rituals, and in Jewish holy writings. No one spoke it in daily life, nor had they for more than a thousand years. That changed with the efforts of Eliezer Ben-Yehuda, who moved to Palestine from Lithuania in eastern Europe in 1881. Ben-Yehuda believed a common language was necessary to unite the thousands of Jews who had moved to Israel from all around the world. He urged that Hebrew be adopted as that language. At first his ideas were ignored, but within a couple of decades, Ben-Yehuda had gained wide support, and the use of Hebrew spread. Ben-Yehuda authored the first modern Hebrew dictionary and created a modernized grammar for Hebrew, creating many new words to describe contemporary ideas and objects.

Languages

Hebrew and Arabic are the official languages of Israel. The form of Hebrew most commonly spoken is Modern Hebrew, which developed in the late nineteenth century. It is based on ancient Hebrew, the language of the Hebrew Bible. Modern Hebrew is influenced by Slavic languages, Aramaic, German, Arabic, and other Jewish languages. Hebrew is used in government, commerce, courtrooms, and schools. Arabic-speaking schools must teach Hebrew to students from the third grade upward.

In 2000, the Israeli Supreme Court ruled that the use of Arabic needed to be expanded. Since that time, road signs, labels on food, and government messages are required to be translated into Arabic. The majority of Israeli Arabs are also fluent in Hebrew.

In addition to Hebrew and Arabic, there are about thirty-three different languages and dialects spoken in Israel. After English, Russian is the most widely spoken. It was brought to Israel by a huge wave of immigrants in the late 1980s and 1990s. Yiddish, a form of German that uses elements of Hebrew, is generally spoken only by older Ashkenazi Jews. Sephardim speak Ladino, a form of medieval Spanish combined with Hebrew. Other languages spoken by Israelis include Romanian, German, and Amharic, which is spoken by Israel's large population of Ethiopian Jews. Almost everyone has at least some knowledge of English, a requirement in all state schools.

The Hebrew Alphabet

The Hebrew alphabet contains twenty-two letters. Five letters have special forms used only at the end of a word. Hebrew is written from right to left, and there are no uppercase or lowercase forms.

Common Hebrew Words and Phrases

shalom	hello, good-bye, or peace
boker tov	good morning
erev tov	good evening
Ma shlomech?	How are you?
bevakasha	please or you're welcome
ken	yes
lo	no
todah	thank you

Common Arabic Words and Phrases

salaam aleikum	hello
sabah al-kheir	good morning
aiwa	yes
la	no
shukran	thank you

Many Faiths

"THE STATE OF ISRAEL...WILL GUARANTEE freedom of religion, conscience, language, education and culture; it will safeguard the Holy Places of all religions." These words from Israel's Declaration of Independence assure freedom of religion in Israel. Everyone there is free to practice his or her religion as that person chooses. Because Israel is where three of the world's prominent religions developed, many different religious practices and traditions are observed there.

Judaism is the majority religion in Israel, with about 76 percent of the population being Jewish. About 16 percent of Israel's citizens are Muslim, 2 percent are Christian, and the remaining are Druze and other faiths. Each of the three major religions has several denominations, or branches, in which different customs and beliefs are practiced.

Opposite: **Jewish men gather to pray at the Western Wall, a holy site in Jerusalem.**

Many Faiths **87**

Judaism

Judaism is one of the world's oldest religions, dating back more than three thousand years. It was one of the first religions to practice monotheism, or the belief in only one god. Jewish belief and doctrines are laid down in the Torah, the first five books of the Hebrew Bible. The Torah explains how the Jews committed to observe God's commandments and to reveal knowledge and acceptance of God to the world. The Talmud, another collection of ancient writings, which are not considered to be scripture, form the religious laws of Judaism. Jewish law focuses largely on moral values and ritual practices. It also gives instructions on how to live one's daily life, including such things as how to dress, eat, and interact with society.

A boy reads from the Torah as part of his bar mitzvah, a coming-of-age ceremony.

The rabbi is a central figure in Jewish life. He or she conducts services in the synagogue, the Jewish house of worship, and is responsible for the education and spiritual guidance of the Jewish community.

A rabbi is considered a teacher, who instructs members of the community and comments on Jewish law.

Branches of Judaism

Over the centuries, Judaism split into different branches. Today, the main denominations are Orthodox, Reform, and Conservative. Orthodox Jews strictly observe the laws of the Talmud and other religious writings. They accept God's word as it appears in the Torah. They do not work on the Sabbath, and they closely follow Jewish dietary laws. Women are not allowed to become rabbis, and they must wear head coverings

Religions of Israel*

Jewish	76%
Muslim	16%
Arab Christian	2%
Druze	1.7%
Other	3.8%

* Does not equal 100% due to rounding

at all times. In the synagogue, men
and women are separated. All prayer
is conducted in Hebrew. About 20
percent of Israeli Jews are Orthodox.

Reform Judaism rejects the strict
interpretations and practices of the
Orthodox Jews. Reform developed in
the early nineteenth century when
European Jews believed they wanted
to live more like the non-Jewish people in their communities. Men and
women worship together in the synagogue, and women are not required
to wear head coverings. Religious
services are often conducted in the
native language of the worshippers,
with little Hebrew used.

Conservative Judaism balances
many of the older traditions of the
religion with the need to adapt to
changes in the modern world. Head
coverings must be worn in synagogue,
but men and women pray together. Services are conducted in
both Hebrew and the native language of the worshippers.

The Synagogue

The synagogue is the Jewish house of worship, or temple. It is a
sacred place, considered the house of God and the Jewish people.

All synagogues include a raised platform, called a bimah, that has a table on which a Torah scroll is unrolled. Rabbis read to worshippers from the Torah. Above the bimah is a lamp or lantern, usually electric, which is lit all the time. The continual light represents the lamps found in the original First and Second Temples in Jerusalem. All synagogues also have a holy ark, where the handwritten scrolls of the Torah are kept. The ark is the holiest spot in the synagogue because the scrolls

Synagogues vary greatly in how they look. This modern synagogue is in Tel Aviv.

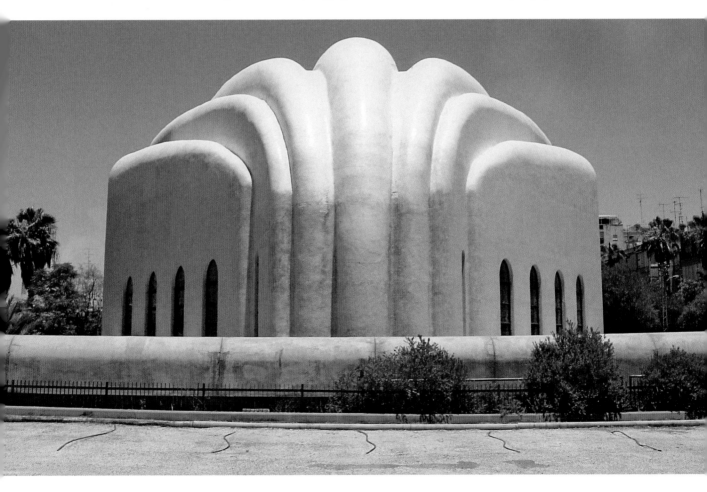

are considered the words of God as given to the Jewish people. A *parokhet*, a fancifully decorated curtain, is placed either outside or inside the doors of the ark. In almost every synagogue in the world, the ark is placed so that the worshippers facing it also face toward Jerusalem.

Jewish Festivals

One of the ways in which Jews of the Diaspora remained linked in faith for centuries was through their celebration of numerous religious and nonreligious Jewish holidays. By observing their rituals, Jews throughout the world were reminded of their common history and remarkable strength.

The Jewish year begins with the holidays of Rosh Hashanah and Yom Kippur, which fall in September or October. Rosh

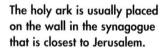

The holy ark is usually placed on the wall in the synagogue that is closest to Jerusalem.

Hashanah is a joyous occasion. The two-day holiday marks the beginning of a new year and the hope for health and happiness in the months ahead. After worshipping in the synagogue, Israeli families often have picnics or go to the beach. Ten days later, Jews observe Yom Kippur, the holiest day in the Jewish calendar. Called the Day of Atonement, Jews ask God to forgive them for any sins they committed during the year. Many Jews fast for twenty-four hours, spending that time in solemn prayer at the synagogue.

Sukkot, the harvest festival, is celebrated a few days later. Families build a *sukkah*, a temporary hut, next to their homes. There, they eat their meals to give thanks for the ending of the harvest season. The sukkah represents the huts of the ancient Jews who wandered the desert for forty years after leaving Egypt.

Simchat Torah ends Sukkot, and Israelis worship, sing, and dance in celebration of the event. The holiday marks the

During Rosh Hashanah, people recite prayers near flowing water and then symbolically throw their sins into the water.

A girl lights Hanukkah candles. One additional candle is lit on each night of the holiday, for eight nights.

completion of the reading of the entire Torah for the year.

Hanukkah, the Festival of Lights, is celebrated in late November or December. For eight nights, people light candles on a menorah, a candleholder with nine branches. This ritual recounts the Talmudic story of how a one-day supply of oil miraculously burned for eight days in the First Temple after the Jews recaptured it from the Syrian-Greeks in 167 BCE. Hanukkah is perhaps the most festive holiday of the year. Families get together to eat traditional treats, and children receive gifts on each of the eight nights.

Purim is a joyous festival that falls in March or April. It celebrates the deliverance of Jews from oppression. Passover is another springtime holiday, a seven-day festival that honors the escape of the Jews from slavery in Egypt. On two nights, Jewish families gather at the seder, a special dinner. Participants read the story of how Moses led the Jews out of Egypt.

Islam

Muslims make up about 16 percent of Israel's population. The holy book of Islam is the Qur'an, whose contents are believed to have been revealed to the Prophet Muhammad by God, or *Allah* in Arabic. This scripture and the teachings of the Prophet Muhammad, which are called Hadith, are used by Muslims to develop Islamic doctrines, ethics, and practices.

The mosque is the Islamic house of worship. The most revered mosque in Israel is al-Aqsa Mosque, which is located next to the Dome of the Rock in Jerusalem. Inside each

A Game of Dreidel

During the week of the Jewish holiday of Hanukkah, Israeli children love to play the game of dreidel. A dreidel is a four-sided top that is spun by a small peg on its top. Dreidels are usually made of wood or plastic. A different Hebrew letter appears on each side of the dreidel: *nun, gimel, hei,* and *shin.* When combined, the letters form the phrase "a great miracle happened here." To begin play, each player is given ten to fifteen game pieces. The pieces are usually raisins, chocolate coins, pennies, or nuts.

At the start of each round, every player puts one game piece into the "pot," the middle of the playing surface. Then each player spins the dreidel. When the top stops spinning, the Hebrew letter facing up tells the player what to do. If it's a nun, the player does nothing. If it's a gimel, the player takes all the game pieces in the pot. If hei faces up, the player takes half of the pieces in the pot. If shin appears, the player adds a piece to the pot. Players take turns spinning the dreidel, and when a player runs out of pieces, he or she is out of the game. The last player with any pieces left is the winner.

mosque is an open prayer area, without any furniture or religious objects. On the wall in front of the prayer area, there is always a mihrab, which points out the direction of Mecca, Saudi Arabia, the holiest city in Islam. An imam stands in front to lead prayer and on Fridays gives a sermon from a pulpit. Many mosques have a small courtyard, where worshippers wash before praying, and a school called a madrassa.

Muslims pray five times a day, facing Mecca. Believers adhere to strict guidelines about food, dress, and the role of women. Gambling, drinking liquor, and eating pork are not allowed in Islam.

Men praying near the Dome of the Rock in Jerusalem. When praying, Muslims always bow in the direction of Mecca, Saudi Arabia.

Ramadan is one of the most important religious seasons or holidays in Islam. Ramadan is the ninth month of the Muslim year. For the entire month, Muslims fast from sunrise to sunset each day, abstaining from eating or drinking anything. Ramadan ends with a one-day feast called 'Id al-Fitr. Families gather to eat sweet pastries and to give gifts to young children. 'Id al-Adha, the Feast of the Sacrifice, is another important Islamic holiday. It celebrates the Jewish prophet Ibrahim, or Abraham. On this day, Muslims pray, and those who can afford it sacrifice sheep, cows, or goats, and at least one-third of the meat is donated to the poor and needy.

Muslims in Jerusalem enjoy a meal after sundown during Ramadan. They will then make their way to a mosque to pray.

Israeli Christians

According to Christian beliefs, Jesus lived in the land of Israel and was buried on the site of the Church of the Holy Sepulchre.

The Prophet Muhammad

According to Muslims, Muhammad is the final prophet of Islam. Muhammad was born in the Arabian town of Mecca around 570 CE. He worked as a merchant, leading caravans in Arabia and as far afield as Syria. He sometimes worshipped or meditated alone in a cave on the outskirts of Mecca. In 610, he had a vision of the angel Gabriel. According to Islamic beliefs, Gabriel delivered God's words to Muhammad and called on him to become a prophet and a messenger to spread the word of God. (After Muhammad's death, these words were compiled into the Qur'an.)

Muhammad began a life of preaching, working to convince his countrymen to turn away from immorality and evil. He urged them to cease worshipping the traditional gods and deities of Arabia, and to worship and submit to the will of God. He slowly developed a group of dedicated followers. His followers were often persecuted in Mecca, so in 622, he moved to the town of Yathrib, which was later renamed Medina, about 280 miles (450 km) north of Mecca. There, he continued his work.

Muhammad organized an army and defeated his enemies in Mecca in 630. On his death in 632, armies of Muhammad's followers swept through the Middle East, Africa, and parts of Asia and Europe. As they conquered each territory, they spread Islam. Within two to four centuries, Muslims became the majority in much of the Middle East. In 640, the Muslims conquered Palestine, which remained under Muslim control for most of the next thirteen hundred years.

Today, there are roughly 1.6 billion Muslims in the world, second only to Christianity, which has about 2.2 billion. Islam is the world's fastest-growing religion.

Christians consider Israel, the birthplace of Christianity, a Holy Land. Most Christians living permanently in Israel are Arabs, but there are also other groups, including immigrants from the former Soviet Union, Armenians, and Greeks.

Almost all denominations of Christianity can be found in Israel. The Greek Orthodox, part of the Eastern Orthodox Church, have a population of two hundred thousand in Israel, making it the nation's largest Christian group. It is headquartered in the Church of the Holy Sepulchre. Other Orthodox branches include Armenian, Ethiopian, Syrian, and Russian. About one hundred thousand Catholics live in Israel. Most are members of the Melkite Greek Church, which traces its origins to Antioch, Syria, in the first century CE. Protestant Christians are represented by Lutherans, Episcopalians, and a growing number of modern evangelicals.

Priests lead a mass in the Church of the Holy Sepulchre.

Most Israeli Druze live in Galilee, Haifa, and the Golan Heights.

The Druze

The Israeli Druze are ethnically Arabs. Their faith, however, is a sect that broke off to form its own branch of Islam in the eleventh century. Because of this, Muslims have traditionally treated the Druze as heretics.

The Druze tend not to be integrated into the larger Arab communities, but they have mixed well with Israeli society. While most Israeli Arabs avoid serving in the military, many Druze have worked in military and security professions. The Druze believe that when a person dies, his or her soul passes to another body. The Druze do not accept converts or marry outside their religion.

There are about 122,000 Druze living in Israel, most in the Golan Heights. Many earn their living by farming.

The Baha'is

The Baha'i faith is a religion that preaches peace, justice, and the spiritual unity of all peoples. According to Baha'is, throughout history a series of divine messengers have established different religions that met the needs of the people of those times. Abraham, Jesus, Muhammad, and Buddha, the founder of Buddhism, were some of those messengers. The Baha'is were early supporters of the state of Israel and believed that the return of Jews to the Holy Land had been predicted in the writings of Baha'i leaders.

The Baha'i Shrine in Haifa

Located on Mount Carmel in Haifa is the Baha'i Shrine, one of the holiest sites of the Baha'i faith. The remains of the Bab (1819–1850), one of the founders of the faith, are housed in the spectacular shrine, completed in 1953. The architectural style of the building incorporates classical Greek and Roman elements, with additional touches of Middle Eastern and Asian design. The gleaming dome of the shrine is made of twelve thousand tiles of fifty different shapes and sizes.

The shrine is surrounded by nineteen tranquil gardens that feature lush cedar and spruce trees, hedges, flower beds, and gravel paths. In 2008, the United Nations World Heritage Committee selected the Baha'i Shrine as an international site of "cultural and natural heritage of outstanding universal value."

Arts and Sports

I SRAEL'S CULTURAL DEVELOPMENT HAS BEEN SHAPED by its diversity of religious and ethnic elements. Returning to Israel after living in other regions of the world for hundreds or even thousands of years, Jews of the Diaspora brought back with them the arts and cultures of their former homelands. Mixing these with the Middle Eastern cultures of Israeli Arabs, Israel has forged its own unique styles in literature, art, the performing arts, and sports.

Opposite: **The Batsheva Dance Company is one of Israel's leading modern dance troupes. They perform all around the world.**

Literature

Many noted early Israeli writers made their way to Palestine around the time of World War I, coming mainly from Eastern Europe and Russia. Shmuel Yosef Agnon (1888–1970) was born in what is now Ukraine and moved several times before settling in Jerusalem in 1924. There, he wrote *The Bridal Canopy* (1922), which established him as a major Jewish writer. Heavily influenced by the Bible, his novels and short stories focus on Jewish life and combine humor with religious themes. In 1966, he won

Yehuda Amichai's poetry is notable for its use of every-day language.

the Nobel Prize in Literature, the only Israeli to have won the honor. Other important works by Agnon are *A Simple Story* (1935) and *Only Yesterday* (1945).

Yosef Haim Brenner was born in Russia in 1881 and moved to Palestine in 1909. Some of his writings feature a mix of Hebrew, Yiddish, Arabic, and English languages. Brenner was killed in 1921 during anti-Jewish riots in Jaffa. Two of his most noteworthy novels are *In Winter* (1904) and *From Here and There* (1911).

Yehuda Amichai (1924–2000) is considered Israel's finest modern poet. Born in Germany, Amichai immigrated to Petah Tikva in 1935 and moved to Palestine the following year. Amichai's work focuses on day-to-day life and wrestles with the issues of the meaning of life and death. His poetry has been translated into forty languages.

Imil (Emile) Shukri Habibi (1922–1996) was an Israeli Arab Christian writer born in Haifa, when it was under British rule. In 1972, he published *The Secret Life of Saeed the Pessoptimist*, which depicted the life of an Israeli Arab using dark humor. It became an immediate classic in Arabic literature.

Dvora Omer, an author of books for children and young adults, was born on a kibbutz in 1932. Her stories and characters are dedicated to the history of Zionism. Omer uses many real-life Israeli heroes such as Theodor Herzl and David Ben-Gurion to tell the story of Israel's struggle for independence. In 2006, she was awarded the Israel Prize, the state's highest honor, for lifetime achievement and contribution to Israeli society.

Imil Habibi wrote about Arab life in Israel. He was one of the most popular authors in the Middle East.

Music

Israeli music is a diverse blend of Jewish and non-Jewish influences that cover a wide range of genres and styles. Classical music is represented by the works of Israeli-born violinists Itzhak Perlman (1945–) and Pinchas Zukerman (1948–), conductor Daniel Barenboim (1942–), and composers Betty Olivero (1954–) and Tsippi Fleischer (1946–). Olivero often incorporates Sephardic influences into her work. In the composition *Achot Ketana* (*Little Sister*), she sets a thirteenth-century Sephardic prayer to music played by violins and clarinet. Fleischer combines Israeli and Arab influences in her classical compositions.

The Israel Philharmonic Orchestra is a leading force in Israeli music. Founded in 1936, the orchestra has performed the works of many Israeli composers.

A World-Class Musician

Itzhak Perlman is one of the world's greatest violin players. Born in Tel Aviv in 1945, Perlman studied at the Academy of Music in Tel Aviv and then moved to the United States to study at the Juilliard School in New York City. He performed his first concert at Carnegie Hall in 1963 and has made frequent television appearances. He has also played special functions at the White House. In addition to his world-famous talents as a classical music violinist, he is an accomplished jazz and klezmer performer. Perlman has conducted several orchestras, including the Detroit Symphony Orchestra and the Saint Louis Symphony Orchestra.

Mizrahi music combines Israeli, Turkish, Greek, Persian, Arabic, and sometimes South Asian elements to form a unique musical sound that is truly the product of Israel. Song lyrics are often taken from Hebrew literature, medieval Hebrew poets, and religious writings. Created in the 1950s

Lively klezmer music is popular at weddings.

by Israeli immigrant communities from Arab countries, the use of traditional Arabic instruments gave the Hebrew lyrics an appealing new sound. In later years, acoustic and electric guitar was added to the instrumentation. Today in Mizrahi music, the use of South Asian instruments, such as the sitar and tabla drum, adds new dimensions to the style.

Klezmer is a folk style of dance music that originated in eastern Europe during the seventeenth century. A favorite musical form of Israel's Ashkenazi Jews, it usually features violins, clarinets, trombones, accordion, and piano. To highlight the expressive and emotional nature of klezmer, players often pepper their performances with sounds of laughing and weeping.

Rap, hip-hop, and rock have long been favorites in Israel. Shabak Samech is considered Israel's first and most popular hip-hop group. Their first album, released in 1995, made them overnight sensations. DAM (Da Arabian MCs) is the first Arab-Israeli hip-hop band. The politically charged lyrics of the music by these three Palestinians often focus on the conflicts between Israel and the Palestinians. Popular rock performers of the 2000s include Synergia, Yoni Bloch, and HaYehudim.

Many Israeli singers have won fame throughout the world. Etti Ankri (1963–) is a singer-songwriter who has been called "the poet of Israel spirituality." Known for her emotional lyrics and singing, she has performed in Israel, Great Britain, the United States, India, and other nations. She has recorded seven albums and has appeared in many movies. Ofra Haza (1957–2000) was an Israeli singer of Yemeni origin. Her ability to blend Eastern and Western instrumentation, arrangements, and dance beats helped gain her fame in Israel, Arab countries, Europe, and the Americas.

Painting and Sculpture

In the early 1900s, artists in Palestine often re-created biblical scenes with images taken from the ancient Jewish communities in eastern Europe. Artists of this period include Samuel Hirszenberg (1865–1908), Ephraim Lilien (1874–1925), and Abel Pann (1883–1963).

Avigdor Arikha (1929–2010) and Holocaust survivor Samuel Bak (1933–) produced important works in the latter part of the twentieth century. Arikha began as an abstract painter, eventually becoming known for his portraits, landscapes, and still lifes. Bak's work often deals with the memory of the Holocaust and how he struggled to come to terms with his own experience.

The Eretz Israel Museum

The Eretz Israel Museum in Tel Aviv holds one of the country's most diverse collections of artifacts that showcase the history and culture of Israel. There are exhibits in archaeology, folklore, cultural history, local identity, and arts and crafts. Established in 1953, the museum is composed of several pavilions, or buildings. Each pavilion focuses on a different subject, such as glassware, ceramics, religious objects, coins, and even the development of Israel's postal service. The museum also has a planetarium.

In the center of the museum complex is Tell Qasile, one of Tel Aviv's most important archaeological finds. Excavations on the site in the 1940s revealed the remains of an ancient port city built in the twelfth century BCE. The city was destroyed in a fire, supposedly ordered by King David in the tenth century BCE.

The museum's garden contains a 1,400-year-old mosaic of birds (above). The mosaic contains many symbols typically found in the Christian faith and art. It is believed that the mosaic was once an ornament in a Christian prayer center.

Israeli sculptors often call upon biblical themes and the struggle for Jewish independence, especially the struggle at the time of the establishment of the state. Important sculptors include Menashe Kadishman (1932–), Israel Prize–winner Yigal Tumarkin (1933–), and Yehiel Shemi (1922–).

Kadishman frequently uses images of sheep, recalling several biblical stories. Many of Tumarkin's sculptures deal with anti-war themes, and Shemi's steel naval memorial at Achziv, near Acre, deals with destruction and human violence.

Israel has many fine art museums, which showcase the works of Israelis and non-Israelis. The Tel Aviv Museum of Art holds a vast collection of classical and contemporary art, including works by Pablo Picasso, Joan Miró, Gustav Klimt, Jackson Pollock, and Roy Lichtenstein. The Museum for Islamic Art in Jerusalem contains a collection of Islamic art from the seventh to nineteenth centuries. On display are silver items, weapons, watches, rugs, jewelry, and illustrated manuscripts.

Dance

Dance is one of Israel's most popular cultural activities. Dance in Israel covers an entire range of styles, from ballet to modern, jazz, and ballroom and folk dancing. The Israel Ballet is a leading company of classical ballet performers. Batsheva Dance Company and the Kibbutz Contemporary Dance Company are modern dance groups. The Inbal Dance Theater in Tel Aviv draws its inspiration from the Bible and blends classical ballet with folk dancing from Yemen. During the summer, the Karmi'el International Dance Festival is held in Galilee. About 5,000 dancers from Israel and other nations perform for crowds of more than 250,000 people. In the fall, the Tel Aviv-Jaffa Dance Festival also presents dancers from

Israel's National School of Art

The Bezalel Academy of Arts and Design in Jerusalem is one of the world's leading art and design schools. The academy was established by Boris Schatz in 1906 with the Zionist goal of creating a national art style that combined Jewish, European, and Middle Eastern practices. In its early years, artists at the school produced works in silver, wood, brass, leather, and cloth.

The school closed in 1929 because of the world financial crisis, but reopened in 1935. Bezalel became a creative haven for many new artists and teachers who immigrated to Israel as the wave of Nazi anti-Semitism swept across Europe. Among the leading artists who studied at Bezalel are photographer Ya'ackov Ben-Dov, sculptor Zeev Ben-Zvi, and woodcut artist and art collector Jacob Otto Pins.

Today, Bezalel offers programs in architecture, fine arts, industrial design, jewelry, photography, animation and film, and art history.

The hora is a common wedding dance.

many countries, including the United States, Spain, China, Japan, and Australia.

The hora is Israel's most popular folk dance and is often performed to accompanying klezmer music. This spirited circle dance is performed at joyous occasions such as weddings. It was introduced in Israel in 1924 by the Romanian Jewish dancer Baruch Agadati (1895–1976). Rina Nikova (1898–1974) was a classical ballet dancer who established the Biblical Ballet group in 1933. Focusing on biblical subjects, Nikova's choreography re-created Israelite dance in biblical times for modern audiences.

Film and Theater

The Israeli film industry dates back to Palestine during the silent film era. In the 1950s, several film studios were established, largely at the encouragement of the Israeli government. Since then, the industry has boomed, especially in the 2000s, when many Israeli-made films won awards at film festivals around the world. Major releases during this time include *Late Marriage* (2001), *Walk on Water* (2004), and *Waltz with Bashir* (2008).

Israel hosts two major film festivals, the Jerusalem Film Festival and the Haifa International Film Festival. The Haifa festival, the first of its kind in Israel, is the country's major movie event. It is held annually during the weeklong holiday of Sukkot.

Israel's active theater scene had its beginnings in 1931, when Habimah, a Hebrew theater group from Russia, moved to Palestine. Since 1958, it has been Israel's national theater. Early Israeli plays dealt with issues of pioneering in the new nation, the Holocaust, and the Arab-Israeli conflict. Hanoch Levin (1943–1999) was a major Israeli play-wright, producing almost sixty works in his career. His subjects varied from the Israeli military and politics to death, the Bible, family life, and marriage.

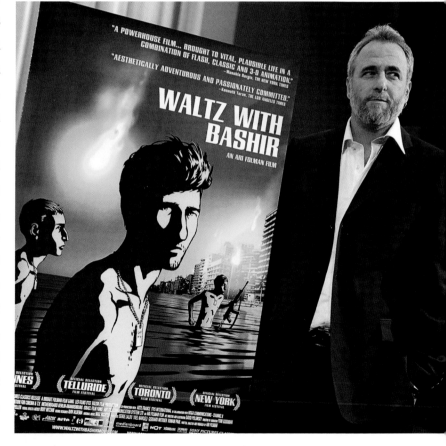

Waltz with Bashir, **directed by Ari Forman, was nominated in 2009 for an Academy Award for Best Foreign Language Film.**

Israel is a nation of sports lovers. The most popular sports are soccer, basketball, track and field, tennis, and swimming. The Israel Football Association oversees all organized soccer throughout the country. This includes more than thirty thousand participants—men, women, and children—playing for about one thousand teams at all levels of competition. Dozens of Israeli footballers play in professional soccer leagues in Europe. On the national scene in recent years, the Maccabi Haifa team has been the top performer, winning the Israeli Premier League championship in 2011.

Israel's Mr. Basketball

Born in Trenton, New Jersey, in 1943, hoopster Tal Brody (second from left) was Israel's first modern-day sports hero. A star player for the University of Illinois basketball team, the high-scoring, slick-passing guard earned All-American and All-Big Ten honors in 1965. That year, Brody was selected by the Baltimore Bullets in the National Basketball Association (NBA) draft. But before the season started, he went to Israel, where he led the U.S. basketball team to a gold medal in the Maccabiah Games, Israel's version of the Olympics.

Brody then decided to pass up the fame and fortune that might have come with an NBA career. Instead, he returned to Israel to help promote basketball. He played for the Israeli Maccabi Tel Aviv team from 1966 to 1980. In the 1977 tournament, he led his team to a historic upset victory over the Moscow Soviet Army team, one of the greatest achievements in Israeli sports history.

Brody not only played on teams for both Israel and the United States, but he also served in the armed forces of the two countries. Regarded as a national hero, Brody was awarded the Israel Prize, the country's highest civilian honor, in 1979. In 2010, he was named as the first international Goodwill Ambassador for Israel, to assist his country in diplomatic relations.

Maccabi Tel Aviv is one of the top basketball teams in the Israel league and among the best in Europe. It has won the Israeli championship forty-nine times and the European championship five times. The Israeli national basketball team has played in twenty-three European Basketball Championships. The team's most memorable moments came in an upset victory over the Soviet Union in 1977 and when it captured a silver medal in 1979.

Israeli tennis players have also made their mark in the world of sports. Shahar Pe'er was ranked number eleven in the world among women in 2011, the highest ranking ever for any male or female Israeli singles tennis player. Andy Ram and Yoni Erlich are a doubles team that has become one of the best in the world. In 2008, the pair won the Australian Open.

Israel has competed in the Olympics as a nation since 1952. In 1992, Yael Arad brought home Israel's first medal, winning the silver medal in women's judo. Since then, Israel has won six medals. In the 2004 Olympics in Athens, Greece, Israeli sailor Gal Fridman won Israel's first and only gold medal, in windsurfing.

Yael Arad celebrates a victory at the 1992 Olympics.

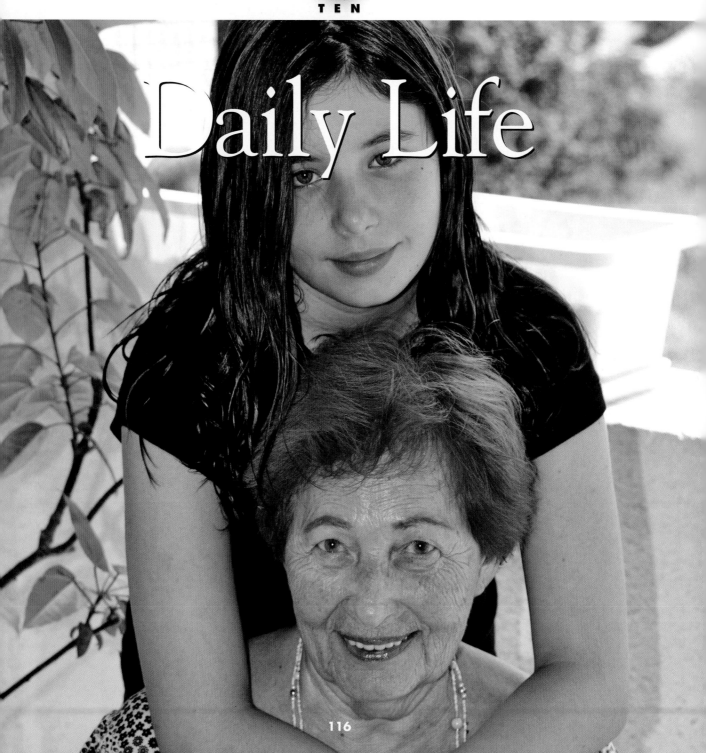

Daily Life

ROUGHLY 90 PERCENT OF ISRAELIS LIVE IN URBAN cities and towns. More than 25 percent of the population lives in the cities of Tel Aviv, Haifa, and Jerusalem. High-rise apartment complexes and tall office buildings are common in major cities, often built alongside ancient sites and historic buildings. Urban dwellers in Israel face the same challenges as residents of most major cities throughout the world. Heavy vehicle traffic, pollution, and shortages in housing and public services are problems in Israel.

Many thousands of Israelis live on settlements, which are Jewish communities built on land captured by Israel during the Six-Day War in 1967. There are roughly 120 settlements scattered throughout the West Bank, East Jerusalem, and the Golan Heights. About 520,000 Israelis live in settlements in these areas. In 2005, Israel removed its residents from all settlements in the Gaza Strip.

Opposite: **An Israeli teenager and her grandmother. About 10 percent of Israelis are over age sixty-five.**

Kibbutz Dovrat was established in 1946. Today, nearly three hundred people still live on the kibbutz.

The Kibbutz

The first kibbutz in Israel was established in 1909 by seven pioneers working near the Sea of Galilee. They were given a piece of land by the Jewish National Fund, the Zionist organization that bought land and financed the relocation of Jews wanting to settle in Palestine. They called their community Kibbutz Degania, and it has been in operation since it was founded.

About 50 percent of Israel's rural population lives and works on kibbutzim. Modern kibbutzim are no longer limited to farming. Today, many kibbutzim have industrial plants that manufacture products such as plastics, textiles, furniture, and bullets. Some engage in high-tech industries, producing telecommunications equipment, medical tools, and irrigation equipment. Other kibbutzim raise money by operating tourist holiday camps and hotels. There are roughly 270 kibbutzim located throughout the nation.

People working on the kibbutz do not receive a salary. Instead, they are provided with housing, medical services, education, and other needs. Members of the kibbutz usually eat in communal dining rooms. They obtain their clothing from the community's shop and have it cleaned or mended at another shop in the community. All children have jobs on the kibbutz and attend special schools that are not part of the Israeli

Israel's National Holidays

Israelis use the standard Western calendar, called the Gregorian calendar, in their daily lives. However, the dates of national and religious holidays follow the Jewish calendar. Because the Jewish calendar has fewer days than the Gregorian calendar, the specific Western dates of Israel's holidays vary each year.

Tu B'Shvat (New Year for Trees)	January–February
Purim (Feast of Lots)	March–April
Passover	March–April
Holocaust Memorial Day	April–May
Memorial Day	April–May
Independence Day	April–May
Jerusalem Day	May–June
Shavuot	May–June
Rosh Hashanah	September–October
Yom Kippur	September–October
Sukkot	September–October
Simchat Torah	September–October
Hanukkah	November–December

school system. Modern kibbutzim offer their members many of the comforts of life outside the kibbutz. Many have swimming pools, sports facilities, libraries, and theaters or concert halls.

Going to School

Israel's school system is divided into five groups: state schools, state religious schools, independent religious schools, private schools, and Arab schools. Arab schools feature instruction in Arabic and a focus on Arab history, religion, and culture. Roughly 70 percent of Israeli children attend the nonreligious state schools.

Children in a classroom in Tel Aviv

Children are required to attend school from kindergarten (age five) through tenth grade (age sixteen). Education is free, but not required, from ages sixteen to eighteen, which is the twelfth grade, the end of high school.

At the end of high school, students must pass a difficult series of national exams, called the *bagrut* (which means "maturity"), in order to attend a university. Students are tested in areas such as Jewish history and heritage, the Hebrew language, literature, art, foreign languages, math, geography, and several sciences.

There are nine universities and several dozen colleges in Israel. Among them are Ben-Gurion University (Beersheba), Bar-Ilan University (Ramat Gan), Tel Aviv University, Hebrew University of Jerusalem, and Open University of Israel in Ra'ananna.

About thirty thousand students attend Tel Aviv University. It is Israel's largest university.

Jewish Burial Customs

According to Jewish tradition, the body of a deceased person must be buried within two nights. A wake, or display of the body, is not allowed because the body must be put in its final resting place as soon as possible. Cremation, autopsies, and donation of body organs are also prohibited. The body must be buried in a simple, unadorned wooden coffin. For seven days following the burial, the immediate family of the deceased person gathers at someone's home in a period of mourning called shivah. The mirrors in the home are covered in cloth, and all mourners must sit on low stools or the floor. Friends and family members visit the mourners, often bringing them food.

Daily religious services are started with the reciting of Kaddish, a special prayer for the dead. Children must

say Kaddish for a deceased parent for eleven months and for other family members for thirty days. Jewish law requires that a tombstone be erected so that the deceased will not be forgotten and the grave will not be disturbed.

Food

Israeli food is a blend of the European, Mediterranean, and Middle Eastern cultures that thrive in the region. It often combines the spiciness of Middle Eastern cuisine with the sweeter flavorings of Europe.

The Israeli diet features an abundance of fruits and vegetables, which are easily available and grown in large quantities throughout the country. Although turkey and chicken form a significant part of the Israeli diet, beef products do not. The lack of good grazing land for livestock is the reason red meat is not an important part of the diet.

Baba Ghanoush

Israeli cuisine is a tasty offering of a wide range of cooking styles from places as far-reaching as the Middle East, North Africa, Europe, the Mediterranean, Asia, and America. One of the most popular and widely enjoyed treats is baba ghanoush, a dish made with eggplant and tahini. Baba ghanoush is usually eaten as an appetizer or side dish, as a dip for pita bread. Have an adult nearby to help with this recipe.

Ingredients

2 medium-size eggplants

Juice from 1 or 2 lemons

1 teaspoon salt

½ cup tahini

2 or 3 garlic cloves, pressed

Black pepper (optional)

Olive oil

Directions

Preheat oven to 350°F. Pierce the eggplants with a fork, place them on a cookie sheet, and bake them for 45 to 60 minutes, until they are very tender. Turn them once while they are cooking. Set the eggplants aside to let them cool. When they have cooled, peel them and put them in a colander to drain for about 30 minutes.

Slice the eggplants into large chunks and mash. Mix with the remaining ingredients except the olive oil until the dip is smooth. If it is too thick, add a few tablespoons of water. Before serving, drizzle with olive oil. Serve with pita bread. Enjoy!

Israelis commonly enjoy several meals during the day. Breakfast often consists of a salad with finely chopped fresh vegetables, eggs, cheese, and fresh bread. Restaurants often add olives, fish, soft cheeses, tuna salad, and avocado to their breakfast menus. Breakfasts always include juices, coffee, tea, and milk.

Later in the morning, many people enjoy a sandwich or biscuit, which is followed by a more filling lunch. The afternoon snack may be another sandwich or a plate of fresh fruit.

Falafel sandwiches are enjoyed as meals or snacks. A falafel consists of fried balls of chickpeas mixed with onions, garlic, and other spices. The mix is wrapped in pita bread and served with tahini sauce, a paste made from sesame seeds. Hummus is a dish made with chickpeas, garlic, olive oil, and tahini sauce. It is usually served with a flatbread, such as pita.

Falafel is popular throughout the Middle East.

More filling offerings include *shwarma* and *shashlik*. Shwarma is spicy grilled cuts of lamb, turkey, or chicken placed in pita bread. It is often served with tahini or hummus, or flavored with vinegar and spices. Chicken shwarma can be served with *toum*, a garlic sauce, or garlic mayonnaise. Shashlik is marinated lamb cooked over a flame. The lamb is marinated overnight in vinegar, wine, sour fruit, or vegetable juice, with herbs and spices added.

Cholent is a stew traditionally served on the Jewish Sabbath for lunch. The main ingredients are meat, potatoes, beans, and barley. Sephardic and Ashkenazi Jews each have their own variations on cholent. Sephardim often use rice instead of beans and barley, and they often substitute beef with chicken. Ashkenazim will usually add a sausage casing or chicken neck skin stuffed with flour and flavorings. Kugel, a hearty noodle or potato casserole, is a popular Ashkenazi dish. For added flavor and aroma, apples, zucchini, sweet potato, or spinach are added to the casserole.

Israeli cuisine offers a wide range of sweet treats. Baklava, a nut-filled Turkish pastry of thin phyllo dough, is served with sweetened syrup. *Bamba*, a favorite of young children, is a soft, peanut-flavored snack. *Kanafeh* and *sambusak*, both of Arab origin, are pastries with a sweet filling. In Israel, sambusak might include potatoes, onions, and peas, or ground chicken.

A man carves shwarma in Jerusalem.

Street vendors offer a wide variety of healthy and tasty foods for Israelis on the go. *Shakshouka* is made of fried eggs in a spicy tomato sauce, and is usually served in the same frying pan in which it was cooked. Thick slices of bread and a side salad are also part of this popular meal. *Malabi* is a creamy pudding that is sold in cups with a thick, sweet syrup and toppings such as chopped pistachio nuts or coconut.

Jewish Dietary Laws

The foods that Jews may eat are spelled out in a set of dietary laws called the kashruth. Foods that may be eaten are referred to as kosher, and those that are not allowed to be eaten are called *treif*. The kashruth lists foods that can and cannot be eaten; how meat must be slaughtered and cooked; and how foods must be served.

Any animal with cloven, or split, hooves may be eaten. The animal must also chew its cud. Cattle, sheep, and goats are allowed, but camels, rabbits, and pigs are not. Only fish that have fins and scales are kosher, such as tuna, salmon, and herring. Shellfish, such as lobster, shrimp, clams, and crabs, are treif. Scavenging birds or birds of prey cannot be eaten. Chicken, geese, ducks, and turkey are considered kosher.

Animals that die of natural causes or are killed by other animals may not be eaten. The slaughter of an animal is done with a quick, deep stroke across the neck with a sharp blade. The blood of the animal may not be eaten and must be fully drained before the meat is prepared.

Meat and dairy foods may not be eaten together. The same pots, pans, utensils, plates, and glasses used in preparing

Islamic Dietary Laws

The Qur'an and Hadith spell out the dietary laws of Islam, noting which foods are halal, or lawful, and which are *haram*, or unlawful. All types of food from the sea and all vegetarian foods may be eaten. Muslims are forbidden from eating the meat of animals that are found dead. Blood, pork, and alcohol are also considered haram. Animals must be slaughtered while mentioning the name of Allah, or God. The body of the slaughtered animal must be hung upside down for all its blood to drain out. Since kosher slaughtering practices also meet these requirements, many Muslims consider kosher foods to also be halal.

or eating the food may not be used for both meat and dairy. Religious households will often have two sets of utensils and cookware: one for meat, and one for dairy.

A Proud People

Despite a history that spans thousands of years, Israel is a young nation. Formed as a homeland for Jews, it also became a home for many others. Among its population are people of many races, beliefs, customs, and religions. Israel's history has been marked by many conflicts with its Arab neighbors. But Israel's hope has always been—and always will be—that a permanent peace can be attained with its neighbors and the Palestinians. In a melting pot of differing hopes and dreams, Israelis of all faiths must work hard and remain optimistic so they may enjoy the freedoms and bounty of the land they call Eretz Israel.

Timeline

Israeli History

Assyrians conquer Israel.	**722** BCE
Alexander the Great conquers Israel.	**332** BCE
The Romans capture Jerusalem.	**63** BCE
Jerusalem is destroyed by the Romans.	**70** CE
Jewish rebels die at Masada.	**72**
Muslim Arabs capture Palestine.	**638**
Christian crusaders recapture Jerusalem from the Muslims.	**1099**
The Muslim leader Saladin recaptures Jerusalem.	**1187**
Ottoman Turks establish control of Palestine.	**1517**

World History

ca. 2500 BCE	Egyptians build the pyramids and the Sphinx in Giza.
ca. 563 BCE	The Buddha is born in India.
313 CE	The Roman emperor Constantine legalizes Christianity.
610	The Prophet Muhammad begins preaching a new religion called Islam.
1054	The Eastern (Orthodox) and Western (Roman Catholic) Churches break apart.
1095	The Crusades begin.
1215	King John seals the Magna Carta.
1300s	The Renaissance begins in Italy.
1347	The plague sweeps through Europe.
1453	Ottoman Turks capture Constantinople, conquering the Byzantine Empire.
1492	Columbus arrives in North America.
1500s	Reformers break away from the Catholic Church, and Protestantism is born.
1776	The U.S. Declaration of Independence is signed.
1789	The French Revolution begins.

Israeli History

Eliezer Ben-Yehuda moves to Palestine and encourages adopting Hebrew as a national language.	1881
The first kibbutz, Degania, and the first modern all-Jewish city, Tel Aviv, are founded.	1909
Britain's Balfour Declaration pledges support for a Jewish national home in Palestine; Ottoman rule ends.	1917
Waves of Jews flock to Palestine as anti-Semitism flourishes in Europe.	1920s–1930s
World War II; the Holocaust claims the lives of more than six million European Jews.	1939–1945
Israel becomes an independent state.	1948
Israel fights the War of Independence against five Arab states.	1948–1949
Israel fights Egypt over the Suez Canal.	1956
Israel defeats Egypt, Jordan, and Syria in the Six-Day War.	1967
Israel battles Egypt and Syria in the Yom Kippur War.	1973
Israel-Egypt peace treaty is signed.	1979
The Palestinian intifada uprising in Israeli-administered areas begins.	1987
Israeli prime minister Yitzhak Rabin is assassinated.	1995
Israel removes all Jewish communities from Gaza.	2005
Israel conducts military operations against Hezbollah in Lebanon.	2006
Israel invades the Gaza Strip.	2008–2009

World History

1865	The American Civil War ends.
1879	The first practical lightbulb is invented.
1914	World War I begins.
1917	The Bolshevik Revolution brings communism to Russia.
1929	A worldwide economic depression begins.
1939	World War II begins.
1945	World War II ends.
1957	The Vietnam War begins.
1969	Humans land on the Moon.
1975	The Vietnam War ends.
1989	The Berlin Wall is torn down as communism crumbles in Eastern Europe.
1991	The Soviet Union breaks into separate states.
2001	Terrorists attack the World Trade Center in New York City and the Pentagon near Washington, D.C.
2004	A tsunami in the Indian Ocean destroys coastlines in Africa, India, and Southeast Asia.
2008	The United States elects its first African American president.

Fast Facts

Official name: State of Israel

Capital: Jerusalem

Official languages: Hebrew and Arabic

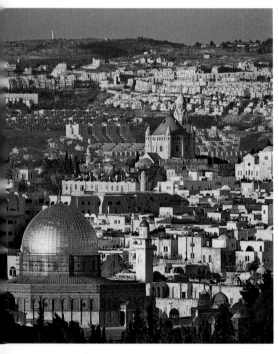

Jerusalem

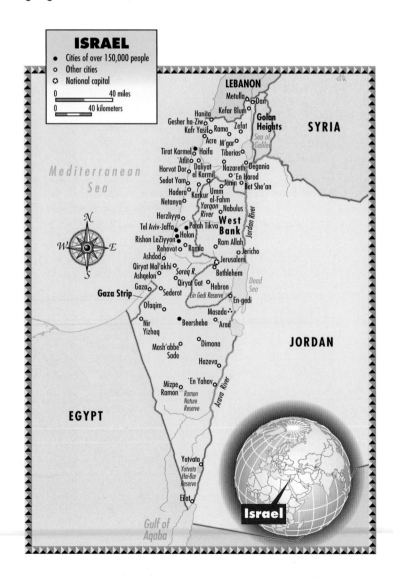

ISRAEL

- ● Cities of over 150,000 people
- ○ Other cities
- ✪ National capital

0 _____ 40 miles

0 _____ 40 kilometers

LEBANON

Metulla
Dan
Kefar Blum
Hanita
Golan
Gesher ha-Ziw
Zefat
Heights
Kafr Yasif
Rama
SYRIA
Acre
M'gar
Sea of
Galilee
Tirat Karmel
Haifa
Tiberias
Atlito
Horvot Dor
Daliyat
Nazareth
Degania
el Karmil
'En Harod
Sedot Yam
Jenin
Bet She'an
Hadera
Karkur
Umm
Netanya
el-Fahm
Yarqon
Nabulus
River
Herzliyya
West
Tel Aviv-Jaffa
Petah Tikva
Bank
Rishon LeZiyyon
Holon
Rehovot
Ramla
Ram Allah
Ashdod
Jericho
Qiryat Mal'akhi
Soreq R.
Jerusalem
Ashqelon
Qiryat Gat
Bethlehem
Gaza
Dead
Gaza Strip
Sederot
Hebron
Sea
Ein Gedi Reserve
En-gedi
Ofaqim
Masada
Nir
Beersheba
Arad
Yizhaq
Mash'abbe
Dimona
JORDAN
Sade
Hazeva
'En Yahav
Mizpe
Ramon
Ramon
Nature
Reserve
EGYPT
Yotvata
Yotvata
Hai-Bar
Reserve
Eilat
Gulf of
Aqaba

Mediterranean Sea

Jordan River

Arava River

Israel

Israeli flag

Dead Sea

Founding date:	May 14, 1948
Founder:	David Ben-Gurion, the first prime minister
National anthem:	"Hatikvah" ("The Hope")
Government:	Parliamentary democracy
Chief of state:	President
Head of government:	Prime minister
Area:	8,522 square miles (22,072 sq km)
Geographic center:	31° 30' N, 34° 45' E
Bordering countries/ territories:	Egypt, Jordan, Lebanon, Syria, the Gaza Strip, and the West Bank
Highest elevation:	Mount Meron, 3,963 feet (1,208 m) above sea level
Lowest elevation:	Dead Sea, 1,388 feet (423 m) below sea level
Longest river:	Jordan River, 199 miles (320 km)
Average temperatures:	January: 43°F to 59°F (6°C to 15°C); August: 72°F to 91°F (22°C to 33°C)
Average annual precipitation:	1.2 inches (3 cm) in the south; 35 inches (89 cm) in the north
Lowest recorded temperature:	7.3°F (−13.7°C) at Tel Hatanim, February 7, 1950
Highest recorded temperature:	129°F (54°C) at Tirat Zvi, June 21, 1942

Western Wall

**National population
(2010 est.):** 7,353,985

**Population of major
cities (2010 est.):**

Jerusalem	773,700
Tel Aviv-Jaffa	403,700
Haifa	265,600
Rishon LeZiyyon	228,200
Petah Tikva	209,600

Landmarks:
- ▶ *Church of the Holy Sepulchre,* Jerusalem
- ▶ *Dome of the Rock,* Jerusalem
- ▶ *Eretz Israel Museum,* Tel Aviv
- ▶ *Masada*
- ▶ *Museum for Islamic Arts,* Jerusalem
- ▶ *Western Wall,* Jerusalem

Economy: Israel's major industries include diamond cutting and polishing, medical electronics, telecommunications, wood and paper products, agricultural technology, potash and phosphates, and computer hardware and software. The tiny nation is a leading international exporter of citrus fruits, including oranges, grapefruits, and tangerines. Major field crops include wheat, corn, and sorghum. Tourism is one of Israel's top sources of foreign currency earnings, with 90 percent of its roughly 2.7 million annual visitors coming from Europe and North America.

Currency: The new shekel. In 2011, 3.39 new shekalim equaled one U.S. dollar.

**System of weights
and measures:** Metric system

Literacy rate: 97%

Currency

Schoolchildren

Theodor Herzl

Common Hebrew words and phrases:

shalom	hello, good-bye, or peace
boker tov	good morning
erev tov	good evening
Ma shlomech?	How are you?
bevakasha	please or you're welcome
ken	yes
lo	no
todah	thank you
Aht medaberet Anglit?	Do you speak English?
slicha	excuse me

Prominent Israelis:

Shmuel Yosef Agnon (1888–1970)
Author

Etti Ankri (1963–)
Singer

Avigdor Arikha (1929–2010)
Painter and illustrator

Menachem Begin (1913–1992)
Prime minister and Nobel Peace Prize–winner

Yosef Haim Brenner (1881–1921)
Author

David Ben-Gurion (1886–1973)
First prime minister of Israel

Golda Meir (1898–1978)
Prime minister

Rina Nikova (1898–1974)
Dancer

Itzhak Perlman (1945–)
Musician

To Find Out More

Nonfiction

▶ Immell, Myra. *The Creation of the State of Israel*. Farmington Hills, MI: Greenhaven, 2009.

▶ Scott-Baumann, Michael. *Crisis in the Middle East: Israel and the Arab States*. New York: Oxford University Press, 2007.

▶ Senzai, N. H. *Shooting Kabul*. New York: Simon & Schuster, 2010.

▶ Seward, Desmond. *Jerusalem's Traitor: Josephus, Masada, and the Fall of Judea*. Cambridge, MA: Da Capo Press, 2009.

▶ Wagner, Heather Lehr. *Anwar Sadat and Menachem Begin: Negotiating Peace in the Middle East*. New York: Chelsea House, 2007.

Fiction

▶ Allred, Alexandra. *Crossing the Line: A Tale of Two Teens in the Gaza Strip*. Logan, IA: Perfection Learning, 2003.

▶ Jacobs, Eli. *Brothers Divided*. Manchester, UK: Devora Publishing, 2005.

DVDs

▶ *Arab and Jew: Return to the Promised Land*. PBS, 2010.

▶ *Israel: Birth of a Nation*. The History Channel, 2005.

▶ *Israel's War History*. CreateSpace, 2009.

Web Sites

▶ CIA World Factbook—Middle East: Israel
www.cia.gov/library/publications/the-world-factbook/geos/is.html
For statistical information on Israel's geography, people, government, economy, and military, as well as an analysis of key international issues affecting the Middle East.

▶ Library of Congress—Country Studies: Israel
http://memory.loc.gov/frd/cs/iltoc.html
To read an overview of Israel's history and social, political, and economic development.

Organizations and Embassies

▶ **Embassy of Israel**
3514 International Drive NW
Washington, DC 20008
202/364-5500
www.israelemb.org

▶ **Embassy of Israel in Canada**
50 O'Connor Street
Ottawa, Ontario K1P 6L2
613/567-6450
http://ottawa.mfa.gov.il

▶ **Israel Ministry of Tourism**
800 Second Avenue
New York, NY 10017
212/499-5650
www.goisrael.com/tourism_eng

▶ **Visit this Scholastic Web site for more information on Israel:**
www.factsfornow.scholastic.com

Index

Page numbers in *italics* indicate illustrations.

Meet the Author

NEL YOMTOV IS AN AWARD-WINNING AUTHOR AND editor with a passion for writing nonfiction books for young people. Bitten by the reading bug at an early age, he learned how books could be the doorway to the wonders of our world and its people. Writing gives him an opportunity to investigate the subjects he loves best and to share his discoveries with young readers. In recent years, he has written books about history and geography as well as graphic-novel adaptations of classic mythology, sports biographies, and science topics.

Yomtov was born in New York City. After graduating college, he worked at Marvel Comics, where he handled all phases of comic book production work. By the time he left seven years later, he was supervisor of the product development division of Marvel's licensing program. Yomtov has also written, edited, and colored hundreds of Marvel comic books.

He has served as editorial director of a children's nonfiction book publisher and also as publisher of the Hammond World Atlas book division. In between, he squeezed in a two-

year stint as consultant to Major League Baseball, where he helped supervise an educational program for elementary and middle schools throughout the country.

Yomtov pulled together the research for this book about Israel from libraries in New York, newspapers, magazines, and Web sites.

He lives in the New York area with his wife, Nancy, a teacher and writer, and son, Jess, a writer and radio broadcaster. He spends his leisure hours on the softball fields in New York City's Central Park and at neighborhood blues clubs playing harmonica with local bands.

Photo Credits